WHY
DID YOU
LEAVE
US SO
SOON?

THE MYSTERY OF
A PREMATURE DEATH

PERRY STONE

WHY DID YOU LEAVE US SO SOON?

Published by Voice of Evangelism Ministries
P. O. Box 3595
Cleveland TN 37320
423.478.3456
www.perrystone.org

Unmarked Scripture quotations are from the
King James Version of the Bible.

Scripture quotations marked NKJV are from the New Kings James Version of the Bible. Copyright © 1979, 1980, 1982 by Thomas Nelson, Inc., publishers. Used by permission.

First Edition © 2024

Printed in the United States of America

ISBN: 978-0-9895618-5-3

Cover Design/Illustration & Layout: Michael Dutton

CONTENTS

DEDICATION

This book is dedicated to every person who has stood at the graveside of a beloved child, dear relative, or close friend and asked, "Why did you leave us so soon?" This might be the lingering question you will ask when you experience the premature death of someone you love and cherish.

Psalm 90:10 tells us, "The days of our lives are seventy years; And if by reason of strength they are eighty years, Yet their boast is only labor and sorrow; For it is soon cut off, and we fly away." This verse describes a sudden passing away, with the person's spirit departing (flying away) from the physical body at death. Some people live beyond seventy to eighty years, while others pass away much too soon, leaving loved ones dealing with grief and sorrow as they are haunted with questions of why.

I began to write this book when my beloved cousin, Louanna Bava Carr, was taken into eternity unexpectedly. I searched for answers to the questions people ask when someone leaves this earth prematurely. This book is for those who have the same questions.

It would be great to enter a time machine and go back to Saturday morning, May 25, 2024 and warn Louanna to avoid that Crystal Springs intersection. But even though we cannot undo the departure of those who are now gone from this earth, perhaps we can learn something to help prevent a future tragedy. My hope is that you will find helpful insights within the pages of this book.

CHAPTER 1

EVERYTHING CHANGED IN AN HOUR

Within an hour, your world can change. And it can change without warning.

For me, it was a beautiful Tennessee morning on Saturday, May 25, 2024. Our daughter Amada had driven up from Alabama and was looking forward to trading her high-mileage Jeep for a new vehicle with a warranty. She, Pam, and I were headed to the dealership. The following day, our family would be leaving early on Sunday morning for a long-planned cruise.

About 10:00 that morning, I FaceTimed one of my best friends who is also my second cousin on my mom's side of the family, Louanna Bava Carr. I told her we were headed out on Amanda's new car adventure. The conversation ended by her saying, "Be sure to send me a picture of the one she picks out so I can approve it."

Louanna's life was focused on family and friends, especially after she retired from her job at the power company. Everybody called her by the nickname LuLu, and we had known each other since we were young. I was eighteen and she was sixteen when she and her dad, my uncle Joe Bava, attended my first revival at Grandad John Bava's church in Gorman, Maryland.

The youngest of ten children, she was labeled the family comedian. If she met a stranger, they didn't stay a stranger for long. Everyone who met her liked her immediately. She made countless friends. At age sixty-three, she was a caregiver for some family members, so she never had been able to get away and come to one of our conferences in Cleveland. Finally, in April of 2023, she was able to attend our International Prophetic Summit. At the four-day conference, our office staff, volunteers, and Pam's close friends fell in love with her and asked her to stay in touch with them.

She had nicknamed me goat, which in sports terminology means "greatest of all time." She thought I was the best preacher out there and often told me that I had taught her so much. She always greeted me with, "Hey, goatie." I countered with, "What's up, sheepie."

In the conversation that Saturday, Louanna mentioned that she soon would be leaving to visit Helen, who is one of Louanna's sisters-in-law whose husband passed away a few years ago. Both of Helen's sons had died in two different vehicle accidents, so there were no children to look after her. Helen lived alone, and Louanna was her caregiver who drove to her home every day to check on her, make sure she had food, buy groceries, pay bills, or take care of whatever Helen needed. Countless times Louanna had said, "I need to live long enough to take care of Helen, my brother David (who had suffered a stroke thirty years earlier), and Pat." Her husband Pat was seventeen years older than Lu.

Before logging off, I said, "Okay, give me a Bava smile one more time before you go!" She smiled her great big smile and reminded me, as she always did, how much she loves us.

A few hours after our conversation, my family was sitting in the lobby of a local car dealership. My phone was on silent, but I noticed that I had received a troubling text message from Pastor Mike Boggs of River of Life Church in Elkins, West Virginia. This is a church that

Louanna and several relatives attend. It read: *"Brother Perry, this is pastor Mike from Elkins. Please call me as soon as possible. There is an emergency concerning your family. Thank you."*

My heart dropped. I knew that Louanna would have been the one to contact me about a family emergency—unless the emergency involved her. Pastor Mike would not be contacting me on behalf of the family unless something had happened to Louanna.

I returned his call and went from anxiety to shock in thirty seconds. Pastor Boggs relayed the tragic information: *"Perry, I hate to be the one to tell you this. There has been a terrible accident. An eighty-year-old man was pulling a cattle truck and carrying nine cows. He ran a red light and t-boned Luanna's car. She was killed instantly."*

Only someone who has experienced this type of tragedy will understand the feeling of utter shock and despair. I wanted more details, which were provided later by Connie, one of Lu's sisters. It took the emergency team two hours to extract Louanna's body from the mangled driver's side of the vehicle. Oddly, she seemed to have no visible outer injuries except some cuts. The initial thought was that the side impact broke her neck and instantly ended her time on earth.

There was no time to think, no time to pray, no time to grasp what was happening. She crossed the veil of eternity with no advance warning. Louanna was a believer, and I know she is with the Lord and with our family members who have gone on before, including her parents. But the reality of her death hit me like a hammer. Louanna was gone from this world, and henceforth I would never talk to her, laugh at her hilarious comments, or see any of her plans for the future come to pass on this earth. I was shocked into speechlessness.

What would the people who depended on her for daily caregiving do without her? What would her surviving brothers and sisters and all the nieces and nephews that she loved and cared for as her own do without her?

SOME FAMILY HISTORY

Louanna and I were both born in the same hospital in Parsons, West Virginia about eighteen months apart. The same doctor delivered us. We share the same family DNA, the Bava Italian lineage. She and I were a lot like my Grandad Bava, who seemed to have known hundreds of jokes and told them daily. We liked the same foods and we thought alike. We were so similar in many ways that I told her I suspected we were twins separated at birth.

Louanna and her husband Pat live on a hill just outside the town of Elkins, West Virginia in a beautiful home that includes a small apartment off the garage area where I stayed when I visited them. Louanna and I, along with our cousin Billy from Virginia, had been clearing out Aunt Millie's house in Parsons, looking for old ministry material (Millie kept it all) and old family pictures and documents. She had thousands of pictures, including some of almost every conference I had conducted. She never missed a conference unless she was physically unable to come in her later years.

Louanna, however, almost made Aunt Millie look like an amateur photographer. Lu had taken and saved around forty-five thousand pictures over the past few years.

Pat and Louanna's home had been built a few miles from a highway between Elkins and Parsons where my parents and I were involved in a serious car accident when I was a toddler. While we were going to Aunt Millie's house, we drove that road where the wreck happened in November of 1961. I told her, "It's chilling to think that sixty-one years ago, we could have died on this road." Pam used to tell me that she loves West Virginia, but she hates those curvy, two-lane roads. Pam gets motion sickness rounding the curves, and the trucks on the roads make her nervous because sometimes they drift over the line into oncoming traffic.

Miles from the area where my family had the car accident that could have taken our lives decades ago, Louanna instantly lost her life in a terrible accident that was not her fault. She was in the worst possible place at the worst possible time.

WHAT HAD I MISSED?

For an entire week, a whirlwind of questions swirled in my head. What had I missed? Why didn't I sense a warning to tell her that she should not go to Helen's that day? Was I not being sensitive to the Holy Spirit to hear His warnings? Should I have taken time to pray safety over her trip that day? Was there anything I could have done to stop it? The entire week, I felt not only the pain of her death, but the guilt of thinking perhaps I could have stood in the gap in intercession, and prayer would have altered the outcome.

When someone you care about dies suddenly and unexpectedly, or when a deadly tragedy suddenly occurs, questions of why and what if can overtake the mind. Why did this happen? Why didn't God protect this person? Why did He allow someone to die in the prime season of their life? Why wasn't I burdened to intercede? Why didn't God give a warning?

My dad, Fred Stone, was blessed with a remarkable spiritual ability that utilized the gifts of word of knowledge and word of wisdom (1 Cor. 12:7-10). He often received visions and dreams, and he could accurately interpret almost any spiritual dream. Many years ago, in a full-color vision, Dad saw his brother Morgan being killed in an accident on a two-lane road in West Virginia. Then he heard the Holy Spirit say, "Today your brother Morgan will be killed by a coal truck between the hours of three and four o'clock p.m. unless you intercede for him."

It was already almost three o'clock, so Dad immediately began to intercede on Morgan's behalf for the next two hours, asking God to send an angel to protect him. Dad said that he felt like he was wrestling with death itself for Morgan's soul.

Later that day, Dad reached Morgan on the phone and told him what had transpired, and how that he had been interceding for Morgan's life and eternal soul. Morgan choked back tears as he confirmed that, indeed, he barely missed being hit head-on by a coal truck. That same truck had hit another car that had been behind his car and the two people in the car were killed. An unusual delay of a few minutes had prevented Morgan's death on the road that day.

Dad had a spiritual gift to know of unseen danger ahead. Several times our family was spared from harm, danger, and possible premature death through Dad's prayers. He prayed every day for the entire family to be protected from harm, danger, and disabling accidents.

I know firsthand that God gives warnings of trouble ahead, and prayer can change the outcome. Throughout the years, I have been warned in advance of coming trouble. But this time, with Lu's accident, I had no burden, no warning dream, nothing. This is the reason I questioned why I had no inkling of the accident that would take Lu's life just hours after we talked that day.

For months before this happened, Lu would ask me numerous biblical questions, especially about heaven. I have written books on the topic of heaven and eternity, all of which she had in her possession. But for some reason, her curiosity was piqued about heaven. She asked questions such as, what happens the moment of death? How old will we look in heaven? Will we know all the people we knew on earth? What happens at the heavenly judgment? Will our sins that are forgiven ever be brought up again? How are rewards given? Can rewards be lost, and how? I was more than happy to answer her questions using whatever biblical insight I had.

In retrospect, it seems unusual that she was so interested in heaven. But for days after her death, I was upset with myself for not having received a warning, so I had to go before the Lord with my own questions.

After seven days, I had some answers. This book was written to share with you what the Bible says and what the Lord showed me about the perplexing question of premature death. If someone close to you has passed away at an age that seems too soon, I hope you will find possible answers and comfort in what you will read.

TAKE ME BACK TO MY CHILDHOOD

Some people suggest that our lives go full circle, from childhood to adulthood, then back to childhood. The desire to go back to childhood is likely based on whether your childhood memories were pleasant or unpleasant. I noticed this with my father in his older years. Dad was raised in McDowell County, West Virginia, and most of his siblings and close family lived in that part of the state until the children grew up and most of them moved away.

In his later years, Dad purchased a small house in Bartley and spent time there visiting people in the area where he was raised and where he had been converted to Christ as a teenager. One of the main reasons Dad chose to do this was in the hopes that he could influence his backslidden half-brother, Morgan, to return to Christ. Morgan had led Dad to Christ as a teenager, but very early in Morgan's walk with the Lord, he became offended at actions of the pastor and his son and refused to ever attend church again. Morgan did not repent and turn back to Christ until a couple of days before he died.

I had written a book about a treasure hunt and hidden a key which, if found, would reward the finder with hundreds of valuable items. I worked on the story during a time of severe trauma and a physical and emotional breakdown. The book took two and a half years to complete. The key was hidden in a place that was special to me, Blackwater

Falls State Park near Davis, West Virginia, where my grandparents had lived. I made several trips to the area, including two with my wife, yet Pam never knew the location of the hiding place.

The trips I took while searching for a good hiding place for the key gave me a strong desire to revisit the small towns in that area, where many of my happiest and funniest memories were made while growing up. This included Christmas each year at the Bava home where our relatives on Mom's side also gathered.

One day my wife jokingly said to me, "I think you're reverting back to your childhood." I researched the idea of reverting back and discovered that when a person has dealt with trauma, they often experience periods of relief by recalling earlier pleasant memories. Not everybody is blessed to have pleasant memories from their childhood, but I'm thankful that I do. Memory recall includes places that trigger a pleasant, peaceful feeling that eases the mind and carries the person back to a time when their life was simple, fun, and joyful.

ALMOST HEAVEN — WEST VIRGINIA

Dad's family grew up in the southern coal mining towns of West Virginia, while Mom's family grew up further north. Robert L. Rexrode, my grandmother's uncle who raised her, started the Davis Church of God in 1930. Davis was a small town, but about eighty people, including children, attended the Davis church in those days. Every person in town who was related to or friends of the Bava family was a member of the church.

Every time we visited my grandparents in Davis, we would drive forty-two miles each way to eat lunch at the Western Steer Steak House buffet in Elkins. Granddad made this trip almost every day. The manager even hung a framed photo of Grandad on the wall, noting that he was their number one customer. A few years before Aunt Millie died, she was hit by a car in front of this same restaurant. Despite being hit on the driver's side, she somehow survived.

When driving through the beautiful Canaan Valley, Elkins, Thomas, or Davis, I am peacefully at home. So many relatives, including a tribe of cousins and their children, live in the area. For much of my life when my grandparents lived there, it was my home away from home. The roads, certain old downtown buildings, local restaurants, state parks, or the waterfalls cause me to step back in a mental time machine and become a kid again.

In October of 2023, I had an overwhelming desire to visit some of those places again. I called my cousin Louanna and asked if she would mind driving me around to different places if I came up to visit. I wanted to see some towns and places I'd never visited. I had never been to the Snowshoe Ski Resort, for instance, but we heard a lot about it growing up.

For four days Louanna served as my tour guide, pointing out different spots, driving me to see family in the area, and eating Burger King Whoppers. She knew many family stories that I'd never heard, and the way she told them was so funny, I had a hard time controlling my bladder from laughing so hard.

I returned a second time in November to clean out our Aunt Millie's house. This precious woman of God passed away in November of 2016, and everything was still in the house, exactly as it was when she had passed. She must have saved every piece of mail she ever received, including bill receipts. Her living room took three days to clean, and Louanna's brother Pete loaded about twenty-five bags of trash to haul off.

I scared Lu and Billy when I heard music that appeared to be coming from upstairs, yet nobody was there playing music. Then I heard a female voice coming from inside a cinderblock garage that was locked and nobody was inside. When I told the two of them what I heard, Louanna threatened to create a new exit in the wall so she could flee.

In our searches, we discovered old black and white family pictures that we had never seen. In dresser drawers were letters, some close to a hundred years old and some written in Italian. We found Great-Grandad Pete's immigration papers from Italy. I collected some old ministry materials, as Aunt Millie had been a ministry supporter since the very beginning, and she saved everything. I found boxes of every magazine, partner's letters, and boxes of cassette messages in every room of the house. I drove home with six large plastic containers, leaving six others stacked in Louanna's garage.

In January I returned to help go through the upstairs rooms and look through thousands of pictures. Millie was like the paparazzi as she would suddenly pull out her camera and snap a shot when you least expected. We accused her of having more pictures than Bayer had aspirin. There were pictures in boxes under the bed, on top the bed, and in the closets. They kept multiplying like Jesus' miracle of the bread and fish.

This was like traveling back in time to rekindle faded memories. Millie had hundreds of color photos of our VOE conferences that covered a thirty-year timespan. I stacked up pictures of former ministry partners who never missed a conference but have gone home to heaven. I knew their names, their spiritual faithfulness, and their volunteer assignments during ministry conferences. The images captured a split-second in time that carried me away to happy events of yesteryear. I was enjoying one of our greatest human gifts—the gift of memory.

MAKE MEMORIES

My wife enjoys family vacations and family time, and she plans vacations a year in advance. She takes a lot of pictures and makes us all dress in the same color clothes for family pictures. She is known for wanting to make family memories.

We all have memories of the past—pleasant ones, unpleasant ones, common ones, and uncommon ones. Common memories fade like a morning fog, and when people remind you of them, your response is often, "I forgot about that." Uncommon memories burn in your mind to the point that you remember exactly where you were when the event happened. You remember where you were when President Kennedy was shot, or when the Twin Towers were hit on September 11.

Unpleasant memories trigger uneasy, restless emotions that cause us to relive that punch in the gut feeling and lock us in a prison of despair. These memories cause wounds that must eventually be healed. Pleasant memories return at times as a gentle reminder that life does have seasons of happiness and joy.

As we age, people will come and go in our lives. Babies become young men and women. One day, young men and women will grow old. We remind ourselves that time is not an ordinary asset but a valuable and limited luxury. If you are blessed to live a long life and your mind remains strong, the one thing nobody can take from you is lingering memories.

Take some time to be with your family while everybody is still here. Take videos and pictures. One day you'll be glad you did. Hug them and tell them you love them. Faith helps us believe and hope helps us hang on. Then there is love. The greatest of these is love (1 Cor. 13).

When death strikes and your closest friends and family are gone from this life, all you have left are memories. The clothes hanging in their closet bring back a place or a special occasion. Their shoes remind you of walks through the neighborhood or a family vacation. Pictures and videos bring back the sights and sounds of thousands of hours together.

Yet, the greatest memory will be the love you shared. The reason you miss them is because you were loved by them, and they were loved by you. Nobody will ever be able to remove that love from your heart.

CHAPTER 2

IF ONLY I WOULD HAVE

For many years I carried guilt for a man's death. It was the 1980s, and Pam was with me as I was ministering at Tony Scott's church in Sylvania, Ohio. After the church service one night, I stayed up late studying. I finally went to bed and closed my eyes, trying to fall asleep. Right away I saw a full color vision of a man standing before me, dressed in brown scuffed work boots, blue jeans that were slightly worn at the knees, and a plaid work shirt. He looked at me for a few seconds and the vision ended.

I opened my eyes and sat on the edge of the bed. I knew that this man attended Pam's church in Northport, Alabama, and that he and his family had been greatly touched by God during a four-week revival. I tried to remember his name and could not. I wondered why I saw him in a vision. Instead of praying for him, I yielded to sleep.

The following day, Pam received a phone call from her sister Shelia, who attended the Northport Church of God. She said, "Pam, I wanted to tell you that Bill Ward was killed in an accident while coming home from work this morning."

As soon as I heard the name Bill Ward, I remembered that he was the man I had seen hours early, before the deadly accident. I asked Shelia to find out how he was dressed. When she called back, I was shocked to hear her describe him exactly as I saw him in the vision.

Months later I spoke to his wife. She had been told the story of how

I saw him in the vision. I will never forget what she said to me: "God must have shown him to you so that you would pray for him. Why didn't you intercede for him? If you had prayed, maybe he would be alive today."

I knew she was right. I had been taught by my dad to follow-up any burden or spiritual revelation with prayer, and to intercede in the situation until you experience a release in your spirit that God has answered. He also instructed that if you see someone in a vision or a troubling dream, begin to immediately pray for their protection.

For many years I wondered, what if? What if I had prayed intently for this man's protection instead of yielding to the weariness of my flesh? God doesn't waste a spiritual dream or a vision. They are given to us for a reason.

THE BIG WHAT IFS

Think about how the world, or even a single life, would have been different if the "what if" questions could be resolved.

What if Eve had resisted the temptation to eat from the tree of knowledge of good and evil? If nobody had ever succumbed to that temptation, all humanity could have lived forever without sin. What if God had found ten righteous people in Sodom? The city would have been spared from destruction. What if the ten Israelite spies had not doubted God's promise and caused unbelief among the people? They would have saved themselves forty years of wandering in the desolate, dry desert and possessed the land decades earlier. What if David had never sinned with Bathsheba and set up her husband to die on the front lines of battle? The sword of the Lord would have departed his house, thus sparing several of his sons from a premature death.

Despite the negative or horrible events, something positive came from each. From Eden's Garden came God's promise of a future

Messiah who would crush the serpent's power (Gen. 3:15). Lot was delivered out of Sodom's fire, and later fathered two sons who formed two biblical nations (Gen. 19:30-38). Out of the forty years of wilderness wanderings came the rise of Joshua and Caleb. Joshua became the leader after the death of Moses, and he led the Hebrew people into the conquest of Canaan and conquered thirty-one cities. David and Bathsheba later bore a son named Solomon, who became one of Israel's most well-known kings.

Your trouble can become the fuel to move you forward in faith. Some of the greatest outreaches in the world that help the poor and needy were birthed out of personal tragedies.

WHAT IS YOUR PERSONAL WHAT IF?

It is impossible to know the number of times that a tragic situation or unexpected death has caused friends and family of the deceased to lament, "Why didn't I see this coming? Why didn't I do something? Why didn't I stop them from going on that trip? Why didn't I spend more time with them? Why didn't I tell them how much I love them?

The simple truth about all of life's what ifs is that none of us can undo what is already done. I questioned myself about Bill Ward and I certainly questioned myself about my cousin Louanna. Her sister asked me, "Why wasn't her angel there to protect her?" My biggest question was, "Why didn't I sense danger in advance?"

I recollect seventeen times throughout my life when I experienced an overwhelming burden that someone I know is going to die soon. It is a feeling of foreboding, a heaviness overloading my spirit and heart, to the point that I am unable to think clearly or focus on work. I often go home and pray. Within a week to ten days, we receive word that someone close to us has died.

In most cases, prayer did not prevent the death of the people. I concluded that the burden could be a spiritual warning to prepare my heart and spirit for the person's departure.

PAY ATTENTION TO SMALL WARNINGS

Sometimes God will send subtle messages to someone in a final attempt to have them change their plans or directions.

The first time my dad received a warning from the Holy Spirit was in 1952 while he was driving. As he approached a narrow, single-lane bridge, he felt a divine presence in the car and heard an audible voice say, "Son, slow the car down. The tie rod is getting ready to fall off this car." At first, he thought someone had gotten in the back seat because the voice was so real. After hearing the same message three times, Dad slowed down as he crossed the bridge. Sure enough, the tie rod fell off and he lost the ability to steer the car.

Nearly a decade later, Dad complained to the Lord about the car accident we had on the road from Davis to Elkins. The Lord spoke to him and said, "I tried to stop you three times, but you didn't pay attention."

Dad remembered the deer that stepped into our lane, stopped in front of the car, and looked at us. He became impatient and drove around the deer. Twice he felt a nudge to take an alternate route, but Mom told him the road was in terrible condition and we shouldn't go that way. Moments later, Dad rounded a curve at fifty-five miles per hour and rammed into the back of a car that had stopped to pick up a hitchhiker. Had Dad waited for the deer to move on its own, or had he obeyed the nudge to take the alternate route, the accident would not have happened.

One Saturday afternoon, I was preparing to drive up toward the Ocoee River when I heard an *inner voice* warning me that I would be involved in a terrible accident if I took the trip. I was already at the front door with my car keys in my hand, but I cancelled my plans and stayed home.

Growing up, on two occasions I witnessed Dad praying loudly and fervently before we took a family trip. In both instances we were involved in a car accident, but there was no injury and very little damage to the vehicle. On one occasion, Mom was driving late at night and the rest of the family was asleep, including Dad who was in the passenger seat. Mom fell asleep while driving and drifted into the path of an 18-wheeler. The driver said he was certain we were going to hit him head on, and he slowed down as much as possible. Instead of hitting him, the back end of our car went over a small embankment on the right side of the road.

The truck driver stopped to assist us and said it appeared that someone picked up our car and put it down over the embankment. I don't doubt that we had angelic assistance that night due to Dad's intense prayers over our trip.

A third example happened years ago when Bill Sheets, a leader in the Church of God, planned to fly to Chicago to receive a doctorate diploma at his graduation from a university. That same weekend, his daughter had scheduled a wedding rehearsal dinner. She didn't want Bill to miss the rehearsal dinner, so she insisted that he have the university mail his diploma. Under pressure from his daughter, he cancelled his flight and chose instead to stay home and attend the rehearsal dinner. The plane he would have been on crashed and killed everyone on board. *The change in his schedule saved him from a premature death.*

Many times, we don't discern the reason for a delay or a prompting of the Holy Spirit, so we ignore it or attempt to hurry through the moment. Doing so can place you in danger's way, or even lead to death.

THE DAY I MIGHT HAVE BEEN KILLED

Years ago, a man named Wayne McDaniel moved to Cleveland, Tennessee. He was a talented painter and enjoyed collecting sports cards, which is my hobby as well. My wife Pam was greatly used of God to lead Wayne back to the Lord, and he became a faithful friend.

One Sunday morning after a church service, we invited Wayne to eat lunch with us at the Holiday Inn's restaurant. After the meal, he asked if I wanted to come to his apartment to look over some ball cards. Amanda was very young at the time, and she started crying uncontrollably, so I decided I should help Pam with Amanda and declined to go. When we drove away from the Holiday Inn, Wayne took the road to the right and we took the road to the left.

Within an hour, we received word that the brakes on Wayne's van had failed while he was driving down the steep hill below the Holiday Inn. He hit the guardrail, flipped his van upside down over the hill, and was hit in the head by cans of paint in the back of his van. Wayne was thrown from the vehicle and part of the van landed on top of him. He died from the accident.

We were in shock and disbelief. I was also hit by the realization that, had I been in the passenger's seat of the van, I also might have been killed or severely disabled that day. I believe the Lord protected me by allowing our daughter to cry so much that I was compelled to help Pam with her.

Here is the sad part. Wayne knew that his brakes were bad and needed to be replaced. He even told people how bad the brakes were, but he continued to delay the mechanical work.

There are times when good people depart prematurely because they ignore potentially dangerous problems. They might drive with tires that have no tread, they might not wear a seatbelt, they might pass on a double line, run red lights and stop signs, or drive in dangerous weather. Breaking natural laws can bring unnatural results—not just for the person engaging in dangerous behavior, but for anybody who happens to be in their path or along for the ride.

PRACTICAL SUGGESTIONS

Are these things simply destined to happen? Or is there something you can do to stop them? Following are some points that I try to practice which might be helpful for you as well.

1. A Sense of Foreboding or Uneasiness

Anytime you sense a burden or an unusual unease in your spirit, you need to stop everything you're doing and pray, preferably in the Spirit. Do not stop praying until the spirit of heaviness lifts. You might be praying over yourself, a family member, or even the nation. This might mean that you need to change plans you've made, but do not proceed if you are uneasy about the plans.

Pray until the burden lifts and you have a complete release in your spirit. That indicates that God has heard, and an answer is on the way. Either the danger has been removed for the person or situation you're praying for, or the situation will not bring the original consequences.

2. Warnings From Other Believers

Do not ignore the warning voices from true believers and prayer intercessors. For several years in a row, some ladies who are powerful intercessors began having urgent warning dreams about our ministry. These included dreams such as fires breaking out on the OCI ministry property, with fires in this context symbolically representing trouble, trials, and persecution. Other dreams included a few people in the form of alligators who were plotting trouble for the ministry and trying to hinder the ministry in various ways.

Later I learned that people had sent warning emails and dreams documented on paper, all of which I should have received. However, a couple of people decided for themselves that the warnings were "stupid" or "not of God," so they intercepted and destroyed these messages and emails before I had a chance to see them.

When someone who is a trusted prayer intercessor gives you a warning from the Lord, do not dismiss it. Even if you don't see any evidence of trouble at that moment, be aware that the enemy is plotting behind the scenes. Pray for understanding of warning dreams and lean upon strong intercessors. If you don't understand the full meaning of the warning, pray fervently until you sense that God has taken charge of the situation. Even though I was not aware of most of these dreams and warnings until after trouble hit, I'm thankful that intercessors obeyed God and stood in the gap.

3. A Warning is a Sign to Pray

My dad was a spiritual dreamer who sometimes received warnings for me, the family, church members, or the nation. He advised that a warning dream is just that—a warning. It is given for one of two reasons. It could be to prepare you for an attack of the adversary that is secretly being planned, so that you are not caught unaware. It could also be given to inspire you to pray against the attack. God will disclose to you the things that are to come (John 16:13). *The warning reveals the possibility, but the intercession can change the outcome.*

4. Pray a Hedge of Protection

When I was growing up, I heard my dad pray one thing consistently. He said, "I ask you, Father, to let no harm, danger, or disabling accidents come to my family." He called our names individually in prayer. He considered this a prayer hedge over the family. I pray the same prayer I heard my father pray. I call the names of my wife, my children, and the grandchildren. I have added an additional request to my prayer: *"Father, do not allow any spirit of premature death to come upon my bloodline."*

The greatest hedge of protection is the power of personal, intercessory prayer. Yes, God is able to do whatever He wants, however and whenever He wants to do it. But there is a spiritual principle where God tells us to ask so that we may receive (Matt. 7:7). Asking requires faith, and sometimes faith requires action (James 2:26). When God answers our prayers, it builds our confidence that God can and does hear us. If God always blessed us without asking, we could incorrectly think we were responsible for the manifestation of the blessing, or we would pat ourselves on the back and praise ourselves for the success.

TROUBLE AT 11,000 FEET

One Sunday night my pilot and I were flying home from Madisonville, Kentucky to the airport in Chattanooga, Tennessee. About fifteen minutes before landing, the right engine went out. I was sitting in front to the right of the pilot, not knowing what happened and fearful that we would drop from eleven thousand feet and become ashes in a ground fire. I imagined angels on stand-by waiting to escort my spirit to heaven upon impact. I mumbled a prayer to remind the Lord that I had much more to do for Him and needed to live longer.

Remarkably, we had only a slightly hard landing. The single left-wing propeller provided enough power for the twin engine 421 plane to make it to the airport terminal. An investigation revealed that bolts came loose and the starter adapter in the right engine broke off, tearing up the gears in the right engine.

The next day, I learned that at least two individuals had prayed for us at the same time that night after experiencing a sudden burden to pray. One was our powerful intercessor, Bea Ogle, and another was

Denise Wright, the wife of the pilot. They sensed danger and began to pray for our protection until we were safely on the ground.

PRAY FOR GOD'S WILL EVERY DAY

The Lord's prayer instructs us to pray, "Thy will be done on earth as it is in heaven" (Matt. 6:10). Christ said to pray for God to deliver us from evil (Matt. 6:13). God had a purpose for us and a foreknowledge of us before we were born (Jer. 1:5). God's will is written in the books of heaven, but His will must be prayed into the earthly realm so that it may be fully manifested in our lives.

Saul of Tarsus, later renamed Paul, was a hardcore Pharisee who defended the law of Moses while enjoying his role as a persecutor of Christians. After his supernatural conversion to Christ, it was revealed by the Holy Spirit that God had called him to be an apostle from his mother's womb (Gal. 1:15). It took a blinding light and the Lord's audible voice to transform him and set him on a street called Straight (Acts 9:8-11).

God has planned your unique life assignments from the womb to the tomb, from your birth to your death. He foreknew you and appointed a time for you to die (Heb. 9:27). Sometimes death is premature. A mother who aborts an infant stops the preplanned will of God for the child's life. Other times, a person can willfully choose a path that leads to a premature death.

Your knowledge that exposes the unseen plans of Satan becomes a secret weapon in your spiritual arsenal. Your intercessory prayer becomes the tool that could save someone's life.

CHAPTER 3

PREMATURE DEATHS FROM DISASTERS

Sudden accidents that result in fatalities can be difficult deaths to explain. Every day, in some city or town, people are dying from vehicle accidents. Compared to the number of vehicles on the road and planes in the air, the number of accident fatalities is low, so we can generally feel safe as we travel.

Some people have a great fear of flying. However, statistics show that, despite the high level of media publicity generated by a plane crash, flying is one of the safest forms of travel. The difference between car and plane accidents is that one plane crash often results in a larger number of fatalities than one vehicular accident. The National Transportation Safety Board noted that in one year, out of 24 million flight hours logged, 6.68 out of every 100,000 flight hours resulted in an airplane crash, and 1.9 of every 100,000 hours yielded a fatal crash.

When a plane crash occurs, whether fatal or not, the Federal Aviation Administration conducts an investigation. When my pilot was flying me back from Madisonville, Kentucky and the right engine went out in midair, the investigation revealed that a bolt came lose on the starter adaptor, resulting in damage to the engine. A later report said that three different planes of the same model had experienced similar failures at nearly the same time.

Airplane accidents can happen for several reasons. Most are from undetected or sudden mechanical problems, storms that bring dangerous weather conditions, or pilot error. Eighty percent of all small or mid-sized aviation accidents can be attributed to human error. The most dangerous times for a small plane are during takeoff and landing.

MAINTENANCE MISHAPS

During a time when our plane was being serviced, our pilot rented a plane from a regional airport. After landing in Texas, the air tower said that another pilot reported smoke coming from one of the engines. Mechanics investigated and found nothing suspicious. We flew the plane back two days later and returned it to the regional airport.

A few weeks later, on December 4, 2004, the same plane was used to transport a group of ministers from a church's denominational headquarters. Upon takeoff, the right engine failed, resulting in a sudden crash that killed everyone except the co-pilot, who miraculously survived and walked away from the crash before the plane caught fire. The co-pilot, a man named Jim, later learned that, prior to the crash, his grandmother in Modesto, California fell to her knees and began praying for him, knowing by revelation of the Spirit of God that he was in some form of danger. Jim and I have discussed that his grandmother's sudden, emergency intercession and appeal to the Almighty to protect him was the key to his life being spared.

On July 26, 2024, members of the Nelon family, known around the world known for their Gospel music, were flying by private plane to join an Alaskan cruise with the Gaithers. Seven people were on board. While flying over Wyoming, a distress signal was sent indicating a problem with the autopilot. Tragically, the plane crashed and caught fire, with the family, friends, and the pilot being taken from earth to their eternal home.

As Christians, on one hand, we rejoice when we know that a believer has entered the kingdom of heaven and is secure in the paradise of God (2 Cor. 12:1-4). However, for those of us remaining on earth, the grief and sorrow overshadow our days and the questions burn within us.

We might question why God didn't prevent the accident. Sometimes the answer is found in the fact that God does not override our human desires or block our human willpower to choose. For example, a flight delay creates its own challenges, such as not arriving at your destination when you're supposed to be there. We can look at the formation of dangerous storms along the path, but sometimes people decide to take their chances anyway. Maybe the plane will arrive safely at its destination, and maybe it will not. This is why we need wisdom and prayer before we make the decision.

BAD CHOICES BRING BAD RESULTS

Three stories stand out in my mind. Years ago, a noted pastor with a thousand-member church was preaching in Kentucky on a Saturday night. He wanted to return home on a small plane after the service that night, because he had to preach in his church on Sunday morning. There was a bad storm along his flight path, and he was warned not to fly that night but to wait until morning. He ignored the advice of airport officials and took off anyway.

A crash resulted in the death of everybody on board, including his son, who was a powerful singer and songwriter. A friend of mine had been invited to fly with them but chose to drive back instead. That decision saved his life, and he is alive in ministry to this day because he made a wise choice.

On August 25, 2001, a pop singer was taping in the Bahamas with six members of her film crew. Her plane crashed shortly after takeoff, killing all on board. I have flown to the Bahamas and ministered on the islands, and I asked the locals in the area about this flight. While there were various opinions, most agreed that the plane was overloaded with people and equipment, causing problems at takeoff because of too much weight. The decision to take off anyway led to a tragic result.

Another tragedy in the Bahamas occurred on November 9, 2014 when the beloved Bahamian minister, Myles Monroe, his wife, and several other ministry leaders perished in a plane crash. The group was headed to a leadership forum hosted by Dr. Monroe. The weather was bad with much fog, but Dr. Monroe felt they should try to make the conference. Poor visibility hindered the pilot from seeing a crane at a shipyard near the Grand Bahamas Airport. The plane crashed into the crane, killing all on board.

In the case of both ministers, bad weather was the culprit. In retrospect, the wise decision would have been to delay the flights until the severe weather passed. If people override wise recommendations and travel when they know it's unsafe, there could be serious consequences.

THE BOAT RIDE FROM HELL

The book of Acts reveals what can happen when someone ignores and overrides warnings. Paul, as prisoner, was taken aboard a ship loaded with slaves and headed for Rome. The Mediterranean region was entering winter, and Paul knew that winter storms on the sea could become dangerous and deadly for anyone traveling by ship. He tried to convince the captain and the boat owner to anchor at a port and not make the journey, as it could turn treacherous.

However, the centurion believed the owner of the ship, and he rejected Paul's wise counsel. They embarked on the journey, and we read that the winds were contrary (Acts 27:4), sailing was now dangerous (Acts 27:9), and finally, the ship hit a violent sea storm, causing the ship to slowly fall apart (Acts 27:14-19). Neither the sun nor stars appeared for fourteen days, and all hope that they should be saved was taken from them (Acts 27:31). Only through prayer, fasting, and the intervention of an angel from God did the people on board survive the shipwreck.

This crisis would have been avoided if the captain and the ship's owner had heeded Paul's warning. But both the ship's captain and the boat owner had a financial investment on the line, as they would be paid for each slave they delivered to Rome. Money meant more to them than safety. Cash was more important than common sense.

It is a human response to question God about why He didn't stop something bad from happening, since He holds the keys to life and death. However, if we break the rules of nature and don't use wisdom or common sense, we risk paying a high price. God will not audibly speak from heaven in a cloud and say, "Yea, I say unto you, do not fly today!" However, He may place an unusual and uncomfortable burden or sense of foreboding in a person's spirit. He may speak through an experienced professional who gives a strong and wise warning. People have perished prematurely because they ignored the warnings.

ACCIDENTS BY FAILING TO DO THINGS THE RIGHT WAY

In the 1970s, when I was attending Kenmore Junior High School in Arlington, Virginia, many high-rise condominiums were being constructed in the Baileys Crossroads area, not far from where we lived. Just before 2:30 p.m. on March 2, 1973, the center section of a 24-story building that was under construction fell to the ground in twenty seconds.

An investigation revealed that the concrete shoring between the 22nd and 24th floors had been removed prematurely. As I recall, when the floors began to collapse, a crane at the top of the building fell and crashed through the center of the building. Thick clouds of concrete dust covered the construction site and surrounding areas. The neglect of proper construction and security measures caused the death of fourteen workers and the injury of thirty-four more.

My dad's mother was Nalvie Stone, and her first husband was Arthur Ball. He passed away in a hunting accident. The story as Dad told it was that Arthur went hunting by himself but never returned home when expected. Some of the men were sent to look for him. When they found Arthur, he had been standing on a brush pile and fell. His gun discharged and shot him on the side of the face. Evidence showed that he did not die right away, but he had been so severely injured that he was unable to move far or call for help.

Arthur was an experienced marksman, but this time he appeared ready to shoot something when he slipped in the brush and shot himself instead. Deaths have occurred with guns when people unintentionally shot themselves or someone else. In a case like Arthur's, it appeared to be a freak accident.

Doing something the right way or wrong way reminds me of the words of Jesus:

> "Therefore whoever hears these sayings of Mine, and does them, I will liken him to a wise man who built his house on the rock: and the rain descended, the floods came, and the winds blew and beat on that house; and it did not fall, for it was founded on the rock. But everyone who hears these sayings of Mine, and does not do them, will be like a foolish man who built his house on the sand: and the rain descended, the floods came, and the winds blew and beat on that house; and it fell. And great was its fall."
>
> – MATTHEW 7:24-27 (NKJV)

The emphasis here is that *storms* are going to come, as it rains on the just and the unjust (Matt. 5:45). It is written, "Man that is born of woman is of few days and full of trouble" (Job 14:1), and "Yet man is born to trouble, as the sparks fly upward" (Job 5:7).

Those who hear and ignore biblical teaching and the life and wisdom of the scriptures are building on sand. This person is called "a foolish man." Those who hear and obey are called "wise" and will be standing on a rock foundation that cannot be shaken or moved.

Always pay particular attention to that one important method God uses to warn you of coming danger or trouble. Listen when the Holy Spirit places a sudden burden in your spirit—a pressure, a signal that danger is ahead or a crisis is in your future. Stop at that moment, pray, and ask God to expose or prevent the danger.

CHAPTER 4

WHY DID MY CHILD PASS AWAY?

There is great joy and anticipation with the approaching birth of a child. Clothes, cribs, and diapers are purchased. Bedrooms walls are brushed with fresh paint and the room is stocked with baby furniture and toys. Yet, many hopes and dreams of raising a child have vaporized with the confirmation of a miscarriage or the death of an infant.

What does Scripture reveal about the spiritual state of children? There has been a debate for centuries about the age at which a child becomes accountable for his or her own sins and decisions. In my younger years, I heard a variety of ages—five, ten, twelve, thirteen, or even older.

In the Jewish faith, age thirteen is significant in the lives of young boys and girls. This is the age at which a Jewish family celebrates the son with a bar mitzvah and a daughter with a bat mitzvah. This translates to "son or daughter of the commandments." Age thirteen is not only considered the age of puberty, but an age at which a young person becomes accountable for his or her own actions.

Scripture notes that when an infant dies, the spirit and soul return to the Lord. The prime biblical example is the death of David's infant son. After the boy was born, he was stricken by sickness and died seven days later. David had fasted for seven days for the child's healing, but when the prayer was not answered, David said, "But now he is dead; why should I fast? Can I bring him back again? I shall go to him, but he will not return to me" (2 Samuel 12:23 AMP).

The child had died, and his spirit left his tiny body and was taken (by an angel) to the paradise chamber, which at that time was located under the earth. David understood that he could not bring the infant back, but he would one day die and be with his son in paradise.

Throughout the New Testament, writers note that Christ continually blessed children. On one occasion Christ revealed how children are assigned their own angels:

"Take heed that you do not despise one of these little ones, for I say to you that in heaven their angels always see the face of My Father who is in heaven."

— MATTHEW 18:10-11 (NKJV)

In this setting, the disciples were asking Christ who was the greatest in the kingdom. Christ brought a little child before Him, then spoke about their angels. These angels are assigned to children, and the angels are continually seen at God's throne. Christ made it clear that heaven is filled with children:

"But Jesus said, "Let the little children come to Me, and do not forbid them; for of such is the kingdom of heaven. And He laid His hands on them and departed from there."

— MATTHEW 19:14-15 (NKJV)

Christ used the simple faith of a child to illustrate to adults the necessity of becoming like a child in your faith (with humility and simplicity) to enter the kingdom of heaven:

"Assuredly, I say to you, unless you are converted and become

as little children, you will by no means enter the kingdom of heaven. Therefore, whoever humbles himself as this little child is the greatest in the kingdom of heaven. Whoever receives one little child like this in My name receives Me."

— Matthew 18:3-5 (NKJV)

The heart of God toward infants and children is evident in the serious warning Christ gave to anyone who would willfully harm a child:

"Whoever causes one of these little ones who believe in Me to sin, it would be better for him if a millstone were hung around his neck, and he were drowned in the depth of the sea."

— Matthew 18:6 (NKJV)

When infants and children pass away, even though they are not alive on earth, they are fully alive and aware in the realm of heaven that we call paradise. This paradise is no longer under the earth, but is now located in the third heaven, where God's throne is located (2 Cor. 12:1-4).

The soul and spirit of departed infants and children are now with the Lord. It is unbiblical for anyone to claim through doctrine or by some strange, alleged revelation that children are in hell. That is contrary to every scripture related to the subject.

THE CHILD'S DEATH

A terrible accident occurred when I was nineteen years old and preaching in Virginia. A five-year old child was playing behind the family's car, and the mother, not knowing the child was there, backed up and accidently ran over her. The little girl was killed. Imagine the mother's unbearable grief.

Pam was friends with a family who planned a gathering at a park. The grandmother was assigned to watch a toddler. In time, they noticed the child was missing. After searching, they finally discovered that the child had wandered off and fallen into a well that was on the property.

These are the kinds of accidents for which people have a hard time forgiving themselves. Yet children, just like adults, are susceptible to tragic and fatal accidents. Loving parents never expect to lose a child. They look forward to seeing the child grow up and one day have children of their own. No parent wants to outlive a child. In these cases that bring such intense grief, there can be no sufficient answer to explain the death of a young child.

Whatever the circumstances, we must maintain faith that every child is in heaven and will be in our future *forever*, if we continue to serve the Lord. Rest assured, we will have an eternity to spend with them and live forever on the New Earth and in the New Jerusalem.

CHAPTER 5

SUICIDE—THE PAINFUL QUESTIONS

Next to losing a child, perhaps the most difficult premature death to handle is that of suicide. Why does a person we love choose to take his or her own life? This is often the most painful death that any family can experience, and it is especially traumatic for children when a parent commits suicide. The effects can last a lifetime.

Suicide brings a gnawing distress that can leave the family with more questions than answers. It leaves those closest to the victim overshadowed with guilt as they question themselves. What could I have done to stop this? Why didn't I see this coming? Why didn't they talk about this? These agonizing and haunting questions linger for months or longer and can have a devastating lifetime effect on a family.

SUICIDE IN AMERICA

Suicide is one of the leading causes of death in the United States. In a recent year, over forty-nine thousand people died by suicide, while as many as 1.6 million adults attempted suicide. Every eleven minutes, one person dies from suicide.

States with the highest suicide rate per one hundred thousand people are Alaska, Montana, Wyoming, and New Mexico, although the total number of deaths are higher in more populated states, such as California, Texas, and Florida. Suicide rates are high on Native American reservations because of their battles with poverty and hopelessness that lead to depression and alcoholism.

Medical professionals say that people commit suicide because they feel like they cannot cope with what seems to be an overwhelming life situation. They may think there is no hope for the future, or they find themselves in the middle of a crisis where they think suicide is the only way out. Some young people have been so severely bullied by their peers, they see suicide as the only way out of their emotional trauma and unbearable pain.

Some of the specific reasons given by the medical community for suicide include sadness and grief, shame or embarrassment, extreme guilt, a sense of not being loved or feeling worthless, feeling trapped and believing their life will never change, intense physical or emotional pain or trauma, and rage or a desire to seek revenge. The latter reason could cause someone to kill another person and then turn the murder weapon on themselves.

Different situations happen in a person's life to cause them to consider or follow through with suicide. Reasons include the loss of a close loved one, especially when there is no support system to help the person deal with grief. Adults can face seemingly insurmountable trouble when they find themselves divorced, unemployed, homeless, or facing severe financial problems. A terminal or painful, lingering illness causes some to want to end their life.

Young people are susceptible to thoughts of suicide when they experience bullying, verbal and mental abuse, or the sudden end of a relationship. We are learning that thoughts of suicide are a side effect of some prescription drugs, including antidepressants. Hormone therapies given to young people who are told they can change their gender have been shown to have devastating effects on their mental health, which has led to suicides.

Every day, millions of people experience one or more of these problems, emotions, and mental strongholds. Not many people want to go through life with a laundry list of problems that seemingly have no end, but most would strongly reject any voice whispering that their only solution is to end their life.

It is important for us to discern the signs of depression and suicidal thoughts in others before it's too late. We can help serve as a restraining force, and perhaps prevent someone's premature death.

When a crisis emerges, most Christians go to their knees in prayer. They run to the tower of friendship and lock arms with close friends. Most eventually rise above the battle that's raging. Isolating oneself from people can open a door to a spirit of depression or oppression. Amid traumatic situations, we might not want to speak to another human being, but these unwelcomed spirits will be glad to use their voice to pour erroneous information and deceit into your mind. At any critical juncture in life, prayer is needed above all else. The person suffering needs to be able to join in prayer with those who love and support them, including someone who will lend their ears to hear and use their voice to encourage.

A SPIRIT OF HOPELESSNESS

Behind the voice of suicidal thoughts is a feeling of utter hopelessness. The Apostle Paul talked about faith, hope, and love—the triplets of the Christian walk (1 Cor. 13). The word hope is found sixty times in the New Testament, and the Greek word means "to expect, to anticipate, to have confidence in."

Faith is used when we ask God for His help, while hope keeps us sustained while we wait on God. Hope is the spiritual tool that allowed Abraham to continue believing he would have a son in his old age (Rom. 4:18). The power of hope is found in Roman 8:25 which tells us, "But if we hope for what we do not see, we eagerly wait for it with perseverance." Hope creates a positive anticipation for something better to come.

Paul's remedy for the Christians in Rome who were being persecuted was to rejoice in hope, be patient in tribulation, and continue steadfastly in prayer (Rom. 12:12). Paul also noted that hope is like a helmet. In Roman times, a military helmet protected the head, while the spiritual application is that it also protects the mind of the person wearing it. Paul noted that hope is a sure and steadfast anchor of the soul (Heb. 6:19).

The value of hope cannot be underestimated. If a person seems to be faltering in their faith, they must hold on to hope. When the disciples failed to cast a spirit from a young child, the father came to Christ saying, "Lord I believe. Help my unbelief." He had faith, but the miracle failed. Yet he held on to hope when he saw Jesus coming toward him. When the father's faith wavered, his hope stepped in. Jesus prayed and his child was healed (Mark 9:17-27).

During one of the lowest points in my life, I received a conference phone call from five minister friends who told me how they were going to pray for me and stand with me until the battle was over. Just that one phone call released a needed dose of hope, knowing that I had friends who cared.

In Proverbs 13:12, we read, "Hope deferred makes the heart sick, but when the desire comes, it is a tree of life." If hope is needed today, but it is delayed or put off into the future, the human soul becomes sick. It can become worn down and weak. The heart and soul will encounter weakness when hope is needed but is nowhere in sight.

Those who have taken their own life hit a wall of hopelessness, feeling that there is no way out of the crisis. Life, joy, and peace are obliterated. Hopelessness has a way of putting a blinder on the mind of its victim, making them unable to see that there is help in God.

When hope is gone, the joy of simple things in life will become meaningless. Conversations seem more burdensome than they are worth. The vexed person will often hide in their room or avoid being around the very people who care the most about them.

My son and I are both satisfied being loners, and we spend a lot of time working by ourselves on our projects. When my son was in his early to mid-teens, he was struggling with rebellion, having become addicted to alcohol and a cough syrup and prescription drug combination that young people in our area were using. A doctor prescribed an antidepressant for him to take. One day he told his mom, "I feel like I want to kill myself." We immediately researched the drug and discovered that one of the serious side effects was suicidal thoughts. Of course we did not want him on that kind of medication, and this is when we began to research natural ways to fight depression.

CAN A SPIRIT BE INVOLVED?

Sin can open the door for spirits from the dark kingdom to enter and begin playing their mind games. But our spiritual adversary will use any and every door as an access point to gain an advantage.

Decades ago, my father was pastor of a church in Hickory, North Carolina. One Saturday night he was up late in the evening preparing for the Sunday morning service. Suddenly, he was overwhelmed by a feeling of depression and sensed a presence with a voice that was putting thoughts in his head. It was telling him, "You are worthless as a pastor. You're not helping anyone. Your church isn't growing. Why don't you kill yourself." The voice was like fiery darts shooting from the doorway into his head. He realized he was dealing with a demonic spirit, and he knew that he had to stand up and audibly rebuke this spirit of suicide. He commanded it to get out of the house. Within minutes the negative presence departed, and peace filled the room.

The following morning, an ambulance was at the neighbor's house across the street. Dad learned that his neighbor had committed suicide in the middle of the night. He believes that this spirit had been attacking the neighbor, who was fighting against it. Then it made its way across the street to harass Dad. When he rebuked it, it returned to oppress the neighbor, who succumbed to its pressure.

The spiritual side of this tragic event is reminiscent of Luke's writings, where he said that, when an unclean spirit leaves a house (person), the spirit will go out looking for another person to enter. When he can't find a new victim, he returns to the location from where he originally came (Luke 11:24-26).

Mark's Gospel made a point about a man who was possessed with a legion of demonic spirits. Mark 5:5 tells us that, night and day, the man was in the mountains and the tombs, cutting himself with stones. The idea of *cutting* himself was coming from the spirit within him that wanted to take his life.

Cutting is seen among some teenagers. There are young people with scars on their arms that serve as evidence of self-inflicted pain. It is used as a way of escaping reality. The spirits in the man who was possessed were tormenting him, which is the pattern of this type of spirit—tormenting the mind and pressuring the person to the point of ending their life.

THE AGONIZING QUESTION

The family and friends of a suicide victim, especially those who are biblically literate believers, are left with a whirlwind of questions. There is always one pressing question on everyone's mind: Did the eternal soul and spirit of the person make it to heaven? Did the person have time to repent? Did their actions negate the possibility of eternal life?

When I was growing up, suicides were rare, and most Christians held the same belief of the spiritual dangers of suicide. After decades of Bible study and experience, I do not believe that one answer fits every situation.

At the heavenly judgment, every person will be judged based upon their level of knowledge and obedience to the truth. The same is true with a person who has taken his or her own life. Someone who takes the life of another person and then takes their own life has placed themselves at a severe level of judgment. This is much different from the person who is already depressed and is taking some kind of medication that makes them even more depressed to the point of having suicidal thoughts.

Christ noted that, at His judgment seat in heaven, there would be "servants, prophets, saints, and those who fear God's name" (Rev. 11:18). These four groups all served God at different levels, and each level receives a particular reward. There is a different type of heavenly paradise for a Christian martyr according to Revelation 6:10. At the judgment, some will receive rewards for their works, and others will have their works burned. They will receive no reward, although their soul will be saved (1 Cor. 3:13-15).

Jesus warned of the damnation of hell (Matt. 23:33). The Greek word damnation is *krisis,* which refers to a tribunal unleashing judicial justice. Christ was calling out the sins of the Pharisees and asking them how they could escape the punishment of hell.

The underworld has different levels. The lowest hell, called Tartarus according to the ancient Greeks, is where fallen angels are now imprisoned in chains of darkness, awaiting the final judgment (2 Pet. 2:4). Luke 16 reveals that there are chambers in the underworld; some were

WHY DID YOU LEAVE US SO SOON?

upper levels and others lowers levels, and they are separated by large chasms. When Judas hanged himself after he betrayed Christ, Peter noted that when Judas died, "He (Judas' spirit) went to its own place" (Acts 1:25). The word place, *topos* in Greek, refers to a specific location or a specific spot. Several old manuscripts read, "that he might go to his just or proper place."

Just as God will judge each person individually at the heavenly judgment, He will also judge each individual who was separated from Him, based upon what was written about them in the books of heaven (Rev. 20:12). There are sins of ignorance and sins of knowledge. This is why the Lord requires much from those who have knowledge of much.

GOD IS THE FINAL JUDGE

It is not possible to say for sure where every person who took their own life will spend eternity. We don't have God's knowledge of circumstances or the condition of a person's heart when they died. We are not the tribunal that decides eternal justice. Most likely we will be shocked that some people made it to heaven and surprised that some people did not.

A person's eternal destination is known by the Father and the Son. Our human nature observes every situation and circumstance, and we draw conclusions based on what we think we know. However, within each person is an area that only God can see with absolute clarity—the thoughts and intents of the heart (Heb. 4:12). Many people struggle with bondages that they want to overcome. They hate the internal struggle between good and evil, light and darkness, life and death. Their heart might be crying out for help. They struggle between cycles of freedom and deliverance. Many cry out to God for deliverance from the power of their flesh, but what if there was nobody to show them the way?

Humans are interested in knowing *why* people do the things they

48

do. But we cannot always read intent. In Greek, the word intent (*anoia*) refers to understanding what is within the mind. A Christian might have the gift of discerning of spirits or word of knowledge, but none are mind readers. Only God truly knows the heart of a person. "Man looks upon the outward appearance, but God looks upon the heart" (1 Sam. 16:7).

These are truths to remember. We cannot undo the past, but we can help determine the future. If you ever face an assault that pulls you toward thoughts of ending your life, remember this. There is *nothing* you are presently dealing with that cannot be changed through the power of prayer. As the great general of faith, Floyd Lawhon said, "There is nothing I have ever gone through that I couldn't pray my way out of."

Troubles you are dealing with today will change in the future. Sometimes trials come upon you suddenly and unexpectedly. If you refuse to give up, and if you surrender the problem to the Lord and let Him handle it, you could wake up one morning and find that the problem is gone as fast as it came. I know this from personal experience. An attack of depression that I encountered in the early 1990s lasted for months. After I told some strong believers what I was dealing with, they prayed for me and were determined not to let the attack continue. I started feeling better right away. Then one day I woke up and realized that all the mental pressure was completely gone. It seemed to flee overnight.

Any wound you now carry that causes you heartache and grief will be healed in time. Remember when you were young and skinned your knees, and your mom would treat the cut and cover it with a Band-Aid. As it started to heal, sometimes you would pick the scab and reopen the wound. It is possible to keep the wound of hurt, betrayal, or grief and heartache open by constantly revisiting and rehearsing it, thereby allowing the stingers to keep shooting through your heart.

If you stop picking the scab, the wounds and heartache will fade with time. But you must choose. You might still remember what happened, but the pain will no longer be there, and one day it will seem like the trouble happened a long time ago.

Before the Apostle Paul's conversion, he was the number one enemy of Christians. He had them arrested and killed. After his conversion, he could always remember his past and was ashamed of the way he treated Christians. His secret of moving forward was found in this verse:

> *"Forgetting those things which are behind and reaching forward to those things that are ahead, I press toward the goal for the prize of the high upward call of God in Christ Jesus."*
>
> – PHIL. 3:13-14 (NKJV)

BIBLICAL EXAMPLES

The Bible reveals examples of individuals who took their own lives through different circumstances. One was a man named Ahithophel whose advice was not taken. He returned home and hanged himself (2 Sam. 17:23).

In another example, Zimri saw that the city of Tirzah had been besieged. He went into the palace of the king's house, set it on fire, and died in the burning house (1 Kings 16:18).

Samson took down the house of the Philistines and died among the ruins when the house collapsed. He said, "Let me die with the Philistines" (Judg. 16:13). In Hebrews, Samson is listed in the hall of faith (Heb.11:32).

Only in the case of Judas does Scripture indicate where the person's spirit went after death. Acts 1:25 tells us that Judas "went to his own place," which was somewhere in the underworld. The Scripture notes that Judas was a thief. Jesus called him a devil and said it would have been better for him not to have been born than to betray the Son of Man (Matt. 26:24).

God alone is the final judge of the thoughts and intents of the heart. But a person should never take his or her own life and risk their eternal destiny. Remember, all things are changeable through prayer and fasting, even the worst of circumstances.

CHAPTER 6

WRONG PEOPLE, WRONG PLACE, WRONG TIME

Years ago, our ministry staff was on a retreat in Pigeon Forge, Tennessee. We were enjoying dinner at the Apple Barn, when my office manager received a message that two of our long-time friends had been killed. I thought it must have been a car accident. Instead, we learned that both had been burned alive in the trunk of a car by drug dealers in Alabama.

The husband-and-wife couple had been part of our ministry team during our earliest conferences in Pigeon Forge. In my opinion, the wife was one of the most gifted vocalists I had ever heard. I thought she sang on par with Whitney Houston. Her husband was a studio musician who played guitar with our conference worship team. They had also served as directors of music at a church in their area.

Her husband, a good-hearted young man, found himself in a struggle with drug addiction. At the time of his death, he owed a couple hundred dollars to a local drug dealer. I was told that, weeks before his death, someone shot the back window out of his car. Despite that, because of his addiction, he planned to stop by the drug dealer's crack house and ask for more drugs.

I was told that his wife, who was not involved with drugs, wanted to ride along with him and be there in case something happened. That decision would turn out to be wrong on all counts—wrong people, wrong place, wrong time.

As information was compiled and the trial eventually unfolded, eyewitnesses testified to what transpired. The drug dealer threated the husband because he owed the debt and because he had filed an earlier police report against him. An argument took place and a fight ensued. His wife had remained in the car, but when she blew the horn, the drug dealer ordered two people in the house to bring her inside. The drug dealer and others in the house tied up the couple with electrical cord and placed them both in the truck of their car. An eyewitness at the house said he heard the female praying in tongues and knew about the Holy Spirit from being raised in church. He refused to participate in the attack out of fear of the Lord.

Two of the guys drove the car to a dead-end road, doused the couple and the car with gasoline and kerosine, and lit the car on fire. The couple passed away in a horrible manner.

I still have music CDs with her singing on the two projects our ministry produced. She was serving as the praise and worship leader at a church when she died at an all too young age of thirty-nine. I imagine the young man finally made peace with God, since he had time to do so before he died. However, their musical giftings that would have blessed so many were erased from this life by very bad decisions.

ABNER — DYING LIKE A FOOL

When David was King of Israel, Abner attempted to overthrow him as king. David's military general, Joab, warned him that Abner was deceiving David and secretly spying on him to seize the kingdom.

Joab made his own decision to call Abner for a meeting, and then assassinated him with a dagger under the fifth rib, which would have placed the dagger in the heart of Abner. In fact, Joab was retaliating against Abner for killing his brother, Asahel, during battle (2 Sam. 3:23-30).

In Hebron, standing at Abner's grave, David lamented his death with the question, "Should Abner die as a fool dies? Your hands were not bound nor your feet put into fetters…" (2 Sam. 3:33-34). The Hebrew word for fool here is *nabal*, and the word can translate as stupid. The Hebrew root word speaks of dishonor or disgrace. Abner was a warrior, so in David's opinion, Abner should have defended himself against Joab since his hands were not tied, or he could have run from the scene since his feet were not shackled. No doubt David was thinking, "Abner, why didn't you do something to stop this from happening to you?"

Solomon asked, "Why should a person die before their time?" He noted two possible causes of premature death—being *overly wicked* and being *foolish* (Eccl. 7:17). The word *foolish* used in this reference alludes to doing something irrational or lacking in judgment. The list of actions that qualify as foolish is endless. Playing with a loaded gun, standing on the edge of a cliff while taking a phone selfie, engaging in road rage, driving through a bad part of town at night, driving while intoxicated, and purchasing illegal drugs can all be defined as irrational or lacking in judgment.

Drug use in the United States is especially concerning, including the overdose of dangerous opioids such as fentanyl. The drug is used legally in hospitals for severe pain management, and it is said to be a hundred times more potent than morphine. It can cause many adverse effects, including respiratory arrest. On the street, fentanyl is often mixed with heroin, cocaine, and marijuana, and in pill form it is pressed to give the appearance of a legitimate prescription drug. A very small amount of fentanyl can kill and kill quickly.

I have known of young people who either purchased or were given a pill to sleep or reduce pain, and it was laced with fentanyl, which caused their sudden death. My son knew someone who had checked into a rehabilitation center, then went back home and within two weeks was found dead from fentanyl.

Our ministry has supported rehabilitation centers that assist people with drug and alcohol recovery. We have seen people who were clean for eighteen months and had their lives on the right track. Then they would return home to their old friends (the wrong people) who pressured them to get high one more time. That one more time was the last time they ever got high, as when the drugs entered their body, it overtaxed their heart and they died.

Illegal drug use is a dangerous game of roulette, a chance you take between living or dying. Anybody who becomes involved with selling or distributing illegal drugs places themselves in danger with local cartels, and in a bad spiritual position with God Himself. One man who was involved in the illegal drug trade decades ago told me that dealers always made an example of those who didn't pay their drug bills. Sometimes baseball bats were used to break the knees of those who could not pay. Anyone who snitched was tortured, cut to pieces with razor blades, or shot as an example to others. Most individuals who become involved in taking or distributing illegal substances find themselves in prison or dying prematurely.

THREE POSSIBLE POSITIONS OF DANGER

The first possible position of danger is the *wrong people*. The adversary has a sly method he uses to insert the wrong influence into a person's life, especially the lives of your children and grandchildren. For example, if there is a personal family crisis evolving, such as a separation or divorce, the child may sense personal rejection. The adversary might fill the void with a person of the same age whose influence leads your child toward rebellion.

Wrong people are not always detected as such in the early phase of friendship. Paul warned not to fellowship with the unfruitful workers of darkness (Eph. 5:11), and not to yoke yourself (be tied emotionally) to an unbeliever. Sin always appeals to the flesh, and a wrong person in your life will always please your flesh but will be repelled by the Holy Spirit in you.

In 2 Samuel 13:3, David's son Amnon had a friend named Jonadab, who is called, "a very subtle man." Subtle is a word for *cunning* or *crafty*. He told Amnon how to deceive Tamar, his half-sister, a virgin, by pretending to be sick and having her come to his bedroom to feed him. Amnon followed his advice and forcibly raped his half-sister, then ordered her from the room because afterward he despised her.

When Tamar's brother Absalom heard of the rape, he secretly plotted to take Amnon's life. Eventually Amnon paid the price and was slain, and the entire episode began with the advice of a crafty, manipulative friend. Paul summed it up best:

> *"Do not be deceived: Evil company corrupts good habits. Awake to righteousness, and do not sin; for some do not have the knowledge of God..."*
>
> – 1 CORINTHIANS 15:33-34 (NKJV)

The second position of danger is to the be at the *wrong place*. There are places that Christians should avoid at all costs. For instance, Christians have no business sitting at bars and trying to make friends with men and women who are controlled by familiar spirits.

In my early years of ministry, a well-known drug dealer converted to Christ. The next weekend he went to a bar, which had been his routine for years. While the bartender was preparing his alcoholic drink, the man stepped into the restroom and looked in the mirror. The Lord spoke to his spirit and said, "You do not belong here anymore." He immediately left the bar that night and never returned. He spent his remaining years serving the Lord.

One of David's mistakes was that, during a time of distress, he left Judea, the home of his tribal roots, and moved into the heart of Philistine territory to a town called Ziklag. While there, enemies invaded and took captive the families of David's six hundred mighty men, seizing their wives, children, and personal possessions. Everyone and everything precious to them was lost.

David nearly lost his own life as his men rose against him. Only God's intervention prevented David's premature death at their hands. David could have avoided this trouble, had he not been positioned in the land of his enemies.

The root cause of his unwise decision was weariness from his personal, thirteen-year-long battle with King Saul, and he knew that Saul would not pursue him if he were living in the land of Saul's enemies, the Philistines. Ziklag was safe from one enemy, but it was a hornet's nest of other enemies. We would call this "jumping out of a frying pan into the fire."

At times, without a person's knowledge, they are at the wrong place; not because of their *choice* but by *chance*. Any person who had been in the same place at that same moment also would have experienced the same negative outcome. Godly people of all ages who love and serve Jesus have perished during mass shootings or other horrifying disasters. One of the parents of a Christian child who died in a school shooting was asked, "Where was God when this happened?" One answer was, "They kicked Him out of public schools years ago." Another parent who was asked the same question commented, "He is where He always is—in control and on His throne, and my child is with Him now." Sometimes a person is trapped in a situation by simply being in the wrong place.

The third position involves the *wrong time*. A good illustration is when Paul was warned by the Prophet Agabus not to journey to Jerusalem because he would be bound and arrested. Paul's response was that he was not only ready to be bound (arrested) but was ready to die for Christ in Jerusalem (Acts 21:10-14). His ministry friends could not persuade him to avoid this journey; therefore, they accepted Paul's desire.

Paul went to Jerusalem, was arrested, and spent much time in Roman prisons. I have wondered how many more people he could have reached, had he been able to continue traveling and ministering to the Gentile nations.

DISCERNING THE DOOR

What might look like an open door is not always the best timing to enter the door. I had been invited to minister in a country south of the U.S. border. It was a good opportunity to preach in churches and to many Hispanic leaders. I came to the knowledge that there had been some serious gang activity in that country. I asked a Christian friend with a federal agency who has access to non-public information what he thought about me making the trip. He gave me some wise advice and suggested that I not make the trip *at that time*, as my recognition from global television could be a risk factor for me in that nation. Using wisdom as we live our life includes the ability to make good choices based on solid facts and to discern and obey warnings.

Years ago, during one of my Israel tours, we had plans to go to Haifa for lunch the following day. For some reason my spirit was troubled about being in Haifa the following afternoon. I requested a last-minute itinerary change, suggesting that we head to the Judean Wilderness and have lunch near the Dead Sea.

The following day, while touring the desert, a bizarre hailstorm with baseball-sized hail struck the city of Haifa. We would have been caught in the middle of this dangerous storm, and our tour buses could have been damaged or our people injured.

You may not know nor need to know the reasons for sensing trouble ahead or having a gut feeling of danger. You simply must follow the leading of the Holy Spirit.

QUESTIONING THE FATAL ACCIDENT

One of the most difficult points to ponder when a loved one is taken in an accident or some other tragic, unexpected situation is the *timing* of the incident. Sometimes just a few minutes or seconds would have made the difference between life or death.

With my cousin, it was about 12:35 p.m. that Saturday afternoon when the intersection light turned green. A vehicle in front of Louanna proceeded through the light when he noticed to his left that a truck pulling cattle was not going to stop. Louanna followed the car in front of her through the green light, and for whatever reason, either did not see the truck or could do nothing to avoid being hit by the time she realized what was happening. The driver of the truck slammed directly into the driver's door of her Buick.

For weeks, I rehearsed over and over the possibilities of a different outcome. What if we had talked just thirty seconds longer on FaceTime? What if she had seen the truck and stopped in time to allow the man to run the light? Just five seconds would have changed the outcome.

Eventually I had to realize that I could drive myself into depression if I kept asking what if. My wife Pam, who was so loving and caring through all this, gently reminded me, "Perry, there is nothing that you can do about it. You can't bring her back. You can't keep rehearsing over and over in your head something you cannot change."

During a time of personal reflection and yes, complaining a bit to the Lord, I heard the Lord speak to me in a gentle voice, "Do you trust me? Do you think this accident was a surprise to me? Do you not think I love her very much?"

I recalled a statement that I had repeated to dozens of grieving relatives and ministry partners. "God knows something about all this that we don't, and He was not caught by surprise. He knew something was coming, and He knew the future". This is a time to trust His purpose, as it is written:

> *"For my thoughts are not your thoughts, neither are your ways my ways, saith the Lord. For as the heavens are higher than the earth, so are my ways higher than your ways, and my thoughts than your thoughts."*

> — ISAIAH 55:8-9 (KJV)

One of my often-used quotes is, "The greatest lesson you will ever learn is to learn your lesson the first time." The second observation is that, instead of repeating the mistakes of others, learn from their mistakes to help avoid your own. But just as important is to listen to the still, small voice and those nudges in your spirit that point you to the right people and the right place at the right time.

CHAPTER 7

TO BE HEALED OR NOT
TO BE HEALED

A great historic revival began throughout America in 1948 and continued into 1955. During these seven years, ten-thousand-seat tent cathedrals were erected in towns and cities across America, and gifted evangelists preached and ministered prayers of faith and healing for the sick.

History records thousands of testimonies of healing. However, every evangelist who emphasized physical healing was restless in their spirit, knowing there were some they prayed for who did not receive a manifestation of healing. The biggest question leveled at every minister involved in this revival was, "Why are some healed while others are not?"

There was a Newsweek poll in which seventy-two percent of Americans who responded said they believe that asking God for healing can result in the person being healed. Despite this high number, entire denominations reject the doctrine of faith healing. They insist that the miraculous gifts of the Spirit ceased in the church in the fourth century when the New Testament was compiled. I will not debate denominational theology here. Instead, I will center on the question of why Christians agree in faith for a fellow believer to be healed, but the person is not healed.

SICK YET STILL BELIEVING

My father had great faith when it came to praying for the sick. He saw many people healed of numerous types of sicknesses and infirmities during over fifty years of ministry. He had great compassion for those who were suffering. The Gospels note that Jesus was "moved with compassion" (Matt. 9:36), which is key to motivating someone to bring relief to those suffering.

Dad was diagnosed with diabetes, and over time the disease did much damage to his eyes, kidneys, and heart. One day I asked him, "Dad, you have prayed for thousands of people during your ministry, and many have been healed through the prayer of faith. Why is it that you have seen miracles but have never been healed of diabetes?"

He replied, "Sometimes it's easier to have faith for others than to have faith for yourself. You also can become so accustomed to an affliction that you learn to live with it instead of persisting in prayer for your healing."

Elisha received a double portion anointing from Elijah, and the Bible records that Elijah saw God perform sixteen miracles. Elisha, after receiving the double portion, saw the miracles double. Yet, we read that Elisha became sick with the illness of which he died (2 King 13:14).

How could a man with such power that his dry bones raised a dead man, not be healed with this same great power? It is a mystery that is not explained in the scripture. However, his sickness in death never took away from his lifetime of miracles.

Dad told me, "When I pass away, you tell people that Fred Stone may have died with a disease, but he died believing that God is a healer, and that He can and does still heal the sick." Dad's own afflictions never hindered him from ministering to others, including praying for the sick.

Many people were raised attending church and listening to different ministers preach. They know what the Bible says, and they know what is required to get to heaven. Yet they die lost in their sins. A minister does not stop believing in salvation, just because some people refuse to receive Christ. Neither should someone reject the doctrine of healing because some may not receive healing.

My friend Pastor Dave Garcia once said, *"We cannot adjust our theology to accommodate a tragedy."* Our circumstances do not change a biblical promise, but our questions often challenge the validity of the promise. Just as some receive Christ as Savior and others do not, some are healed but, at times, others are not.

Years ago, an individual had a great ministry of seeing God heal people. Thousands of documented miracles occurred in the ministry. When asked why some were not healed, the response was, "I cannot answer that, as it is a question that I have wondered my whole life. However, I saw many terminally ill people who were unsaved and knew they were going to pass away. They gave their life to Christ and followed Him until the end of life. Their healing came when they passed from this life to heaven, and the good news is that they gained eternal life." There is no death, sickness, sorrow or pain in heaven (Rev. 21:4).

There are many theological theories that attempt to explain why people who believe that God can and does heal, are not healed. I will share my experience, biblical research, and observations in hopes to shed light on this question. These are just a few possible reasons that may or may not relate to your own situation.

1. The Influence of Unbelief

The unbelief of the person who needs healing, or of a church, or even a town can hinder a healing from manifesting. Jesus healed "all who were oppressed by the devil" (Acts 10:38), except for those in His hometown of Nazareth. Matthew 13:58 says that He could do no mighty works there because of their unbelief.

Unbelief will stop your prayers from being answered, as God answers prayers of faith and not prayers of doubt. Notice the comments that James made concerning prayer and doubt:

> *"But let him ask in faith, with no doubting, for he who doubts is like a wave of the sea driven and tossed by the wind. For let not that man suppose that he will receive anything from the Lord; he is a double-minded man, unstable in all his ways."*
>
> — JAMES 1:6-8 (NKJV)

Speaking doubt is the manifestation from our spirit of a deep well of unbelief. When we waver, we have divided judgment, or the inability to make up our mind. Even a jury must be unanimous to bring a verdict. A divided jury is called a hung jury, which ends in a mistrial. If you vacillate between believing and not believing, the result will cause your prayer to be stuck and your answer to never manifest.

Many years ago, a well-known healing evangelist was ministering under a large tent and seeing outstanding miracles through prayer. He asked those who needed healing to place one hand on their body and one on the chair in front of them as a point of contact. A woman who had cancer on her face placed her hand over the cancer. After prayer the cancer fell off into her hand and her face was restored to normal. She began to speak words of unbelief, saying, "I can't believe this! I can't believe this! This is not possible!" She touched her face again with the cancer in her hand, and immediately the cancer reattached to her jaw.

The woman began to weep and people heard her say, "What my faith took off, my unbelief put back on."

The first spiritual law of receiving something from God, including healing, is to have an absence of unbelief in your heart and spirit, and an absolute assurance that God is going to answer according to His Word. Otherwise, you could void that for which you are asking.

The disciples received a rude awakening when a team of nine failed to cast an unclean spirit from a young boy. Jesus told them that their prayers failed because of their unbelief, and that it would take a combination of prayer and fasting to remove their unbelief (Matt. 17:21).

I have observed many prayers for healing that end with wavering. Seekers cry out for a miracle in faith, receive prayer at the altar, then walk out of the room confessing doubts, uncertainties, or unbelief. Sometimes unbelief becomes the strongest barrier to a person's healing, as the rule of answered prayer tells us to ask in faith without doubting in your heart. Instead of unbelief that hinders a prayer for healing, come with a firm expectation, knowing that healing is yours because it's a promise in the Covenant.

2. The Influence of If

Prayer that uses the conjunction "if" can cause a hindrance to a miracle. Millions of prayers have been offered to God on behalf of someone lying in a hospital bed or suffering from a terminal illness. A sincere individual might offer up this kind of prayer, "Lord, if it be your will, raise them up." I once asked Dad, "In all your years of ministry, did you ever see anyone healed after people prayed, 'Lord, if it be your will?'"

He paused to think about it and said, "My goodness, son. I don't think I ever saw anyone healed when people used those words."

Praying "if" places a doubt on the promise of healing. Praying with an "if" is passive and weak. When the leper came to Jesus, he said, "Lord, if you will, heal me." Jesus replied, "I will" and he was cleansed (Matt. 8:2-3). Jesus removed the if.

Since healing and salvation are both covenant promises, praying "if" would be like praying for the salvation of a sinner by saying, "Lord, if it is your will to save them, then save them." It is God's will that all men would be saved; no ifs about it. To receive salvation, we confess with our mouth that Jesus is Lord and believe in our heart that God raised Him from the dead (Romans 10:9). With the heart one believes unto righteousness, and with the mouth confession is made unto salvation (Romans 10:10). This is God's biblical promise.

We have many healing promises that include:

- "By His stripes you were healed" (1 Pet. 2:24)

- "He Himself took our infirmities and bore (carried away) our sicknesses" (Matt. 8:17)

- "Who forgives all of your iniquities and heals all of your diseases" (Psa. 103:3)

- God revealed His covenant name in Exodus when He said, "I am the Lord that healeth thee" (Exod. 15:26). *Lord that healeth* is Jehovah Rapha, one of the compound Old Testament Hebrew names that identifies a characteristic of God.

With many promises of God's ability and power, we must ask in faith without wavering. You might say, "I did believe, and they were not healed." Don't give up on believing for healing. If the person you prayed for was a true follower of Christ, they were healed when their spirit left their body and entered paradise. For a Christian, at death, they have reached the primary goal—to finish their race strong in faith and cross the finish line at heaven's gate.

Israel desired food in the barren wilderness. They asked, "Can God furnish a table in the wilderness?" This was a simple question; however, David noted that they sinned by provoking God. They tempted God in their hearts and spoke against Him when they asked this (Psa. 78:17-19). God told them that He would provide; it was a promise. Yet, they questioned the promise, and that entire generation of unbelievers traveled in circles for forty years, falling short of what could have been.

Once you ask in faith, never speak contrary to your prayers. You don't want to abort your breakthrough with a confession of unbelief.

3. The Influence of Divided Agreement

Sometimes a pastor asks everyone to "agree in prayer." However, often the prayer becomes divided instead of united in agreement. Jesus taught that two or three people can agree for what they shall ask, and the Father will hear and answer them (Matt. 18:19). The Greek word *agree* is *sumphoneo,* from where we derive the English word *symphony.* In a musical symphony, everyone must be playing in the same key. To agree in prayer means to pray the same thing in agreement, or to be in one mind and one heart in agreement.

When a congregation is asked to pray for someone's healing, they are often told to pray, but not always instructed on *what* or *how* to pray. Here is an example of what can occur, demonstrating four different types of prayers ascending to God.

Some will pray, "God, heal them and raise them up for your glory." Another group might say, "Lord, we ask that your will be done for this person." A third group might pray a passive prayer of, "Lord, you see them. Help them Lord," without asking God for anything specific. A fourth group in the church might even be praying, "Lord, don't let them suffer. Take them to heaven to stop their suffering."

These prayers are not, in any way, a prayer of agreement. But since they cover all the options, one group will be able to declare that their prayer was answered.

When two or three agree, they must be in spiritual unity concerning what they are praying for and confessing. They must hold fast their confession, nothing wavering (Heb. 10:23).

Sometimes people can agree in prayer but become divided in their hearts. Prayer must be birthed from the heart and not just the mouth.

If a double-minded person cannot receive anything from God, imagine what it sounds like in heaven where prayers are received, when one congregation of four hundred people prays in four different directions.

We must come into one mind and one accord, as they did in the upper room at Pentecost (Acts 2:1-4). Unified prayers of agreement according to the promises of God's Word become answered prayers.

4. The Influence of the Human Will

Throughout my decades of ministry, I have known many wonderful, godly men and women who were suddenly stricken with a terminal disease that cut their lives short. These Christians believed the Bible and attended a church that taught and practiced praying for the sick, as admonished in James 5:15, "And the prayer of faith shall save the sick and the Lord shall raise them up...." However, they still passed away after suffering.

Moses revealed that God has a name: your healer (Exod. 15:26). Peter taught that Christ provided healing atonement on the cross, and by His stripes we are healed (1 Pet. 2:24). While these promises are true, there must be evidence of personal faith and a strong human will to maintain that faith, especially amid a barrage of negative medical reports. It can be difficult when the circumstances that we hear and see counter the truths that we *believe.*

During the last two years of my father's life, he was on dialysis. The last two weeks before he died, he was hospitalized for several days. Then he was taken to a nursing facility where he died within a week. It was difficult for us. However, Dad's will (his choice) was to transfer to heaven. His personal will overrode any prayers of faith that would have asked God to heal him or extend his life.

When it comes to living or leaving, if the afflicted person is in covenant with God, the Almighty considers their desires, which reveal the will of their heart. The Apostle Paul could have died on numerous occasions, and a few times, he thought the time for his departure had arrived. But Paul lived on, as God had more for him to do in the ministry. When he knew that his time of death had arrived, he wrote, "I am now ready to be offered, and the time of my departure is at hand..." (2 Tim 4:6). He was ready to go, and he knew that his life's clock had expired.

There have been times when the prayers of people have kept a sick person alive, but privately the person's desire was to die and be with the Lord. Yet they continued to allow people to pray for their healing. In one family, the person suffering asked the family to stop praying for them to remain on earth. Within a short time, the person passed away.

When someone dies from a disease, we may never know the prayers they prayed or the untold desires of their heart. God may have heard and honored their prayer by taking them to be with Him.

5. The Influence of Confessing Your Faults

One of my early spiritual mentors was a noted minister who served as a Bishop and Overseer in our denomination. The following is a story he shared with me which demonstrates the importance of confessing your faults when requesting prayer for healing.

In the 1970s, I was a teenager living in Virginia. A minister who served in a state position with the denomination had been diagnosed with a fast-spreading cancer. Upon hearing the report, thousands of people began to intercede for his healing. Despite much prayer, his condition worsened. Eventually he became so weak that he was confined to bed at his home.

I will never forget the summer night during a state camp meeting on the church campground when an ambulance pulled up to the side of the open-air tabernacle. Thousands of people were gathered that night, and all watched as men carried a cot from the ambulance with this precious minister lying on it. He had asked to be brought to the service that night.

The cot was placed on the platform and the minister was handed a microphone. His voice was weak, and he struggled to even whisper. Suddenly he began singing, "Through it all, through it all, I've learned to trust in Jesus, I've learned to trust in God…" To the amazement of those present, his whisper became stronger and stronger, until he sang loudly, clearly, and with great energy. The entire place exploded in worship. The moment was so powerful that the night speaker for the camp meeting stated that he believed this man had been healed.

However, a few weeks later, he passed away. I remember taking care of his young son the day of the funeral. I was close friends with his older son, also a teenager. Honestly, I was a bit confused. How could so many people be praying for healing, and yet he was not healed in this life? What about his voice when he sang, almost supernaturally? Then a man of God publicly stated that he believed the minister was healed. I was not the only one struggling for an answer.

Many years later, the state bishop who had served in Virginia during that time moved to another state and invited me to preach a weeklong revival. During this time, the bishop told me the following story.

He explained that the minister was a good, godly man and a great preacher. But there was something he didn't understand and sometimes criticized. There were times when an anointed minister prayed for people, and they would be so overcome by the presence of God, they would fall under the power of the Holy Spirit. The bishop said, "I remember hearing him criticize this manifestation and say he didn't believe it was necessary."

He continued, "During a state meeting, while he was bedridden, the Lord spoke to me and said that, if this minister will admit he was critical and ask God to forgive him for his statements, God will manifest healing in his body. The Lord strictly told me not to tell him that, but to give him an opportunity to confess from his heart. I took a group of ministers, and we went to pray for the brother.

"We gathered around his bed and began to pray. In a few moments, the presence of God struck his body. He pulled the covers back, stood up, and began to worship. At that moment I asked him, 'Is there anything—anything at all—that you feel you need to confess before the Lord?'

"He replied, 'No.' I asked him the same question in different ways, and he replied, 'Not that I know of.' Suddenly, he sat down, the glory lifted, and he did not have the strength to get back up from the bed again. I wanted to tell him what the Lord said, but the Holy Spirit completely restrained me. The Lord wanted him to examine his own heart. His opinion concerning this manifestation would not keep him out of heaven, but it would prevent him from being healed."

The importance of confessing a fault is penned in the book of James. He wrote, "Confess your faults one to another and pray one for another that you may be healed" (James 5:16). The Greek word for fault refers to a false step, a slip, an error, or an unintentional or intentional transgression of some type. James noted that if we confess our faults to the elders and are anointed with oil during a prayer of faith, God can and will heal us.

James added, "And if they have committed sins, they shall be forgiven" (James 5:15). Remember, James was not addressing sinners; he was addressing believers in the church. When we confess a fault or a sin, God gives instant relief to us through that confession. True repentance and confession also allow us to receive healing.

In the church, Christians often preach against sins such as fornication, adultery, lying, stealing, or certain bondages. However, the most often overlooked sins are not the sins of the flesh, but sins of the human spirit. These are sins that you cannot see, but they defile our faith and our inner spirit. Such sins include bitterness, strife, reviling, and unforgiveness. These must always be confessed and cleared from the heart and spirit of believers before any type of healing can manifest.

During Christ's ministry, healing and forgiveness went hand in hand (Matt. 9:2-6). Christ's physical scourging was for our healing, and the cross purchased our redemption and eternal life. Both salvation and healing require faith and confession, and confession of sins and faults will remove them from our heart and spirit, thus enabling the Lord to perform His marvelous work.

PAUL'S THORN

At times, even with sincere prayers for relief, there may be a higher purpose for why God allows a negative circumstance to persist. Paul wrote of having a thorn in the flesh, a messenger (an angel) of Satan to buffet and harass him. This was an evil angel assigned to stir up difficulty everywhere Paul ministered.

Paul listed twenty-two different hindrances that he dealt with throughout his ministry, and most were caused by this messenger of Satan. Wicked city and religious officials were demonically inspired to persecute, arrest, abuse, and harass him (2 Cor. 11:23-28). On at least three occasions, he prayed and asked God to remove this thorn. The Lord told Paul that He would not remove it, but He would extend a supernatural measure of grace to enable Paul to endure each crisis and be victorious in faith.

Paul knew that the satanic messenger was appointed with a mission to prevent him from being exalted (in pride) because of divine revelations he was receiving, including one incident where he was caught up and enjoyed a personal tour of the heavenly paradise in the third heaven (2 Cor.12:4). Cycles of trouble from within and from without knocked the pride out of Paul and kept him walking in humility. This thorn in his flesh was frustrating, and sometimes it was physically painful. However, God permitted it for a specific reason.

Before Paul's beheading, he believed God could have "delivered him from every evil work and preserved him unto his heavenly kingdom" (2 Tim. 4:18). Yet, he did not ask the church to pray for his deliverance from prison or death. When the time came, he was prepared and ready to go, finally being freed from the evil angel that was his thorn in the flesh.

There are hundreds of testimonial videos of near-death experiences. Many have one pattern: when someone sees heaven or paradise, they do not want to leave the place and come back to earth. All were disappointed when they returned to their physical body on earth, and they lived in high anticipation of their permanent return to heaven.

We must settle in our hearts that those who are with the Lord are in perfect peace and health, and they do not desire to return to earth. They are "the spirits of just men (righteous people) made perfect" (Heb. 12:23). These righteous souls know that, if you are a believer, you will be coming to join them when your life on earth is finished. This is our hope, the resurrection of the dead in Christ (1 Thess. 4:16-18).

If, for whatever reason, we do not see a manifestation of healing or a miracle that extends a person's life, this does not and never will negate the fact that God can and does heal through prayers and acts of faith (James 5:15).

Lazarus became sick and died. Four days later, Christ raised him from the dead. However, he did not live forever in his human body. His time was extended until he died a second time, and that time he was not raised. He will be resurrected when the Lord descends from heaven and the dead in Christ shall rise (1 Thessalonians 4:16).

God can heal us and add years to our life, as seen in the narrative of King Hezekiah, who had fifteen years added to his life (Isa. 38:5). However, we all have an appointment with death (Heb. 9:27). We will live forever only when our spirit makes a final exit from our body. Earth's kingdoms can keep you on the planet only so long. The kingdom of heaven, however, plans on keeping you forever.

CHAPTER 8

WHY IS ONE TAKEN AND THE OTHER LEFT?

For those who are well versed in Scripture, when we hear of "one being taken but another one being left," our attention is drawn to Matthew 24, where Christ warned that at His return, "two (people) would be working in a field, one would be taken and the other left" (Matt. 24:40). In this chapter, I am not referring to the return of Christ. I am speaking of a tragic accident where someone loses their life, while another individual survives.

Why does this happen? Was the other person's survival the will of God? Was it a matter of being at the right place during a bad situation? The Bible gives an interesting narrative to illustrate the death of one and the survival of another.

TWO MEN TARGETED WITH DEATH

In Acts 12, two men had been arrested. Both were leading apostles among Jewish believers. Both lived in Jerusalem. Christianity was exploding in growth during this time. To please the anti-Christian leaders, Herod Agrippa ordered the arrest of James, the brother of John (who penned the book of Revelation). Later Herod arrested Simon Peter, the chief apostle to the Jewish branch of the young Christian church.

WHY DID YOU LEAVE US SO SOON?

James was immediately executed, much to the delight of the Pharisees and the anti-Christian mobs, all of whom resisted the spreading of the Gospel throughout Jerusalem. This happened eleven years after the stoning of Stephen, the first Christian martyr mentioned in scripture (Acts 7:58).

As the people cheered James' death, Herod, who was seeking higher poll numbers among the religious Jews, set his sights on Peter, who was a much bigger threat to Jerusalem's religious hierarchy than James. Peter was sentenced to prison, with orders given to prepare for his public humiliation and execution after Passover (Acts 12:4).

The same night that Herod planned to parade Peter before a hostile audience, an angel of God released Peter from his prison chains. The prison cell door opened, and Peter walked out the iron gate that led to the city. He went directly to a home where believers were in deep prayer for Peter's release.

The plans for Peter's premature death were cancelled in the court of heaven and interrupted by an angel on assignment. Later, this same angel was sent to execute a judgment against Herod. The same man who was drunk on murdering Christians died after being eaten by worms (Acts 12:21-23). Pallbearers carried Herod's corpse to a final burial tomb.

Why did James die and Peter live? The philosophical debate would lead to questions such as: Did God love Peter more than James? Did Peter have more favor than James? Searching through scripture, there could be several possibilities for why Peter's life was supernaturally spared. Perhaps the primary reason was because of a prophecy.

THE POTENTIAL POWER OF A PROPHECY

There is *protective power in a personal prophecy*. A personal prophecy is a word concerning your future that is given by a credible Christian, under the divine inspiration of the Holy Spirit. It will generally confirm something God has already told you about His plans for your future. Sometimes people give personal prophecies that are not from God, but from their own spirit. Your spirit needs to bear witness that the word is accurate.

Jesus had spoken a personal prophecy to Peter concerning his future, and it is recorded in the book of John:

> "I assure you, most solemnly I tell you, when you were young you girded yourself [put on your own belt or girdle] and you walked about wherever you pleased to go. But when you grow old you will stretch out your hands, and someone else will put a girdle around you and carry you where you do not wish to go. He said this to indicate by what kind of death Peter would glorify God. And after this, He said to him, Follow Me!"
>
> – JOHN 21:18-19 (AMP)

At the time Christ said this, Peter was possibly around thirty-five to thirty-eight years of age. Based on this word from Jesus Himself, Peter knew that he would live to an old age and be led to a place he did not want to go. Peter was probably between sixty-two and sixty-seven years of age when he was led to his death *by crucifixion*. He was carried (by his enemies) where he did not wish to go, thereby fulfilling Christ's words.

This prophecy became Peter's protective hedge that kept him from facing a beheading at the hands of Herod Agrippa I. Peter was asleep in prison when the angel struck him to wake him up. I believe Peter slept because he knew that the time of his departure had not come, and God would deliver him (Acts 12:7).

Peter's supernatural escape from death and prison happened because he needed and received divine protection to continue his earthly, God-ordained assignment. This attack from Herod was a satanically inspired interruption in which the adversary hoped to use the ego of Herod to kill Peter to take out the head leader of the Jewish believers. Thus, the enemy would disrupt the plans of God in Jerusalem. But Christ's prophecy became his protective hedge.

Personal prophecies are important if they truly come from God. Paul taught his spiritual son Timothy to use the personal prophecies that he had received (from Paul) to fight his spiritual battles (1 Tim. 1:18).

When we were flying and lost an engine on the plane, great fear overwhelmed me, as I knew from studying past plane accidents that a lost engine was the source of countless fatal crashes. I wondered if I was about to be another statistic on the FAA's list or be mentioned on the news as a television evangelist who died in a tragic plane crash. I could just image the local newspaper stories.

However, once I got over the shock, something rose up in me. At that time, we had begun construction on the Omega Center facility, which the Lord had instructed me to build. I said to myself and to the Lord, "I cannot go to heaven yet, because God told me to build a gathering place, and He would not take me out before it's finished!" I began to fight for my future with *specific scriptures, several personal prophecies, and words the Lord had dropped in my spirit in previous years.*

THE POTENTIAL POWER OF PRAYER

James was arrested and beheaded so swiftly that the believers in Jerusalem might have had no time to call an emergency prayer gathering to intercede on his behalf. With Peter, word spread among Jerusalem Christians to meet at a set location to pray for Peter's safety and release. There is no record of what they prayed or how long they prayed, but we know they focused on Peter's release.

In the wilderness, Israel provoked God by forging a golden calf, dancing before it naked, and worshipping the shiny object for bringing them out of Egyptian bondage. In His anger, God told Moses that the people had corrupted themselves, and He was going to destroy the entire nation and raise up a new nation through Moses.

At the time, Moses was eighty years of age. He likely had no desire to become a father and raise a bunch of children. He told God that, if He didn't forgive their sin, and if He chose to blot out the Israelites from the book, to blot him out, too. Moses became an advocate and reminded God that He was bound by covenant to the descendants of Abraham. Through Moses' intercession, God repented, meaning that He changed His mind and course of action. Instead of death, He gave Israel a second chance and spared them from divine annihilation (Exod. 32). The power of prayer and intercession cannot be underestimated.

Throughout my life, from childhood to adulthood, I have experienced miracles through the power of someone's emergency intercession. I know firsthand that prayer changed the outcome of events or disasters that could have led to my premature death. Many of you can vouch for the power of prayer, and there's no way to know what might have happened had people not interceded to stand in the gap on your behalf.

THE POTENTIAL PLACE OF THE POSITION

What does this mean, "the place of the position?" In the Bible, when the tower of Siloam collapsed, eighteen people died (Luke 13:4). It was not because they were sinners sentenced to death by a heavenly judicial decision. *They were people who were at the wrong place at the wrong time.*

After the terrorist events of September 11, 2001, I received powerful testimonies of many Christians who took the day off from work because they followed a strong burden not to go into the city or the

Twin Towers to work that morning. In one church, most of the members worked in the area of the World Trade Center. That morning, almost none of them showed up to work on September 11. They followed an inner burden instead of their rational thinking, and their lives were likely saved that day.

There may be times when you sense that something is wrong, but you can't put your finger on the reason. *Never override that gut feeling that something is not right.* Sudden inner burdens are often clues from the Holy Spirit that danger is ahead, and the situation requires your immediate attention and prayer.

Where you are positioned—at a stop light, in a plane, in your car— could save your life or take your life. People have survived plane crashes because of the seat they were sitting in. Many of us have known or heard about a young driver who flipped a vehicle or hit a tree because of careless driving. In some cases, one or more people died, while one or more lived.

People make decisions that can have devastating consequences. A reckless driver might not be involved in an accident the first ten times he runs a red light or a stop sign. But the eleventh time could result in someone's death. A drug user might take illegal drugs for years before unknowingly taking a pill that is laced with deadly fentanyl. Driving while intoxicated is also a potential death trap.

The hope for people who make poor decisions is to have someone interceding for their protection and salvation until an answer comes. It is only through the mercy, grace, and power of God that their behavior will change and their life might be saved.

Sometimes God will motivate the spirit and mind of a person not to take a trip or to take a different route on the road. He might cause a delay to keep the person in place. Don't be too busy, too impatient, or too rational and make the mistake of overriding the still small voice.

IN SUMMARY

In the accident, the house fire, the violent shooting, or whatever the case may be, why did one die and another survive? The answer might not always be known on earth, but it will be known in heaven. In the meantime, here are some things to remember.

1. War Over Your Assignment

God planned a long-term ministry assignment for Peter. This apostle would oversee the congregations of Jews who received Christ as Messiah. He supervised the Jerusalem church, which was the headquarters of Christianity. Jesus had changed his name from Simon to Peter, which in Greek means "a rock." When you know that you or a family member has a God-ordained assignment, use it to battle for someone's future and even their life.

David was under a thirteen-year assassination attempt from King Saul. David needed protection from God because he was assigned to be the next king of Israel. He prayed this prayer that he would not die before his time:

> "He weakened my strength in the way; He shortened my days. I said, O my God, take me not away in the midst of my days: Thy years are throughout all generations."
>
> – PSALM 102:23-24 (ASV)

Moses became depressed and wanted to die (Num. 11:15). Elijah became despondent and burnt out with ministry, to the point that he asked God to take his life (1 Kings 19:4). Both men were stressed out with their present situation. Yet God had great plans for both. Moses penned the first five books of the Bible, the Torah. Elijah even has a future assignment to be one of the two witnesses during the tribulation (Rev. 11).

I have survived a car wreck, a plane engine failure, near disasters, and a desire to quit. But I believe God still has a ministry assignment on my life that I must fulfill. When I have completed that assignment, He will transfer me from earth to heaven.

Your retirement from secular work *is not an indicator* that your life on earth will end soon, or that God is finished with you. He might have an assignment and many more years of life for you, so use them wisely.

2. Prayer Can Alter the Outcome

There is no question that prayer can alter negative outcomes. The prophet Isaiah informed Hezekiah to prepare his house and family for his impending death. The king humbled himself and asked God to extend his time on earth. In response, God reversed the set time of the king's death and added fifteen more years to his life (2 Kings 20). This serves as an example that sincere prayer can add more years to a person's life.

3. There Is a Time to Go

At one point, Paul believed he would go to Jerusalem and die for the Gospel. He made the trip but did not die (Acts 21:13). Upon his arrival, Paul was arrested and spent years, off and on, confined in prisons. He even wrote four epistles in the Bible from prison. He was not killed in Jerusalem, but years later he was beheaded in Rome.

Satan made several attempts to kill Jesus. The first time was as an infant, when Herod sent soldiers to slaughter all male infants two years of age and under (Matt. 2:16). The family escaped to Egypt for a season.

The second attempt was when Satan suggested that Jesus jump from the high pinnacle (wall) at the Temple, telling Him that angels would protect Him. This would have been outright suicide (Matt. 4:5-6). Jesus refused to jump at the devil's challenge.

A third attempt occurred in Nazareth after Jesus' sermon offended the local attendees. He was forced from the town's synagogue and led by a mob to a hill where angry men attempted to shove Him off a cliff. Christ turned around, passed through the midst of His attackers, and walked to a nearby town to continue ministering (Luke 4:29-30). Several times the Pharisees plotted to stone Him, but they failed. Violent storms erupted on the Lake of Galilee; yet even a boat full of water could not sink His small ship (Luke 8:23).

However, after forty-two months of supernatural protection, John noted that Jesus' hour had come (John 13:1). Shortly thereafter, Jesus was arrested, beaten, imprisoned for the night, then crucified.

Just as with Christ, there is a difference between BTH and ATH—*Before the Hour* and *After the Hour*. If you pray, obey God, and remain sensitive to God's voice, He can and does provide a hedge for protection because the hour (of death) has not yet come. God can and will preserve us for our life's assignment so that we can complete His will in our lives.

Death is an appointment, and Christ alone has the keys of death (Rev. 1:18). His death and resurrection gave Him authority over death. This is where trust comes in. The door of death is opened or closed by Christ. When the time comes for the death of a believer, He opens the gate of heaven, and we enter the heavenly celestial world. Once His followers enter, none want to return to earth.

THE ETERNITY QUESTION

Years ago in our town, a young Christian girl who did not drink alcohol went out with college friends to a club in Chattanooga. Everybody drank except her. She said that her reason for going was to be the designated driver and keep her friends from driving home intoxicated.

Late that night, she drove her friends back home. They were involved in a head-on collision before they made it home. The Christian girl was killed, while her friends survived with minor injuries.

That is a tragedy we simply cannot explain. But we can ask ourselves this question. What if the other people in the vehicle who were without a redemptive covenant had died in their sins? The eternal outcome for them would have been far different from that of their born-again friend. If they die spiritually lost, there is no hope left for them.

If your child passed away and was serving the Lord, consider this. *You will see your child again.* Your child is with the Lord in paradise, awaiting the resurrection of the dead in Christ. Despite our grief and sorrow, we still have hope.

We all need to be aware that we have a soul and spirit that is eternal. Your soul and spirit represent the real you. The body in the casket at the funeral is an earthly shell. There are two final places for an eternal destination. Choose eternal life with Christ.

At the Rapture, we are told that one will be taken and the other will be left (Matt. 24:40-41). The principle of one taken and another left can be seen each day, when through unexpected circumstances, one person's life is taken while another person remains on earth.

In the parables of Christ's return, the theme is always to watch and be ready for His unexpected return. We must live as though He might come today, even though He might delay until tomorrow. We must treat life and death the same way. We might live a good, long life. But we could also leave this world before the sun rises in the morning. Living in this manner is not living a life of fear; it is living with the expectation of eternity.

Eternity is not waiting for the oldest person in the church to arrive. Eternity can sweep down a highway or into a hospital room and snatch up the youngest among us. Keep a repentant heart and live in right standing with God, so that when Christ returns or when your appointed time comes, you are ready to be taken into His presence, no matter how you go.

GOING BACK TO PERSONAL PROPHECY

Paul reminded Timothy to battle the adversary using the prophecies that had been spoken over him (1 Tim. 1:18). At times a prophetic word has no condition attached that requires a person to take specific actions for the fulfillment to occur. The only requirement is to walk in faith and obedience according to God's will.

At other times, in order to walk in a prophetic assignment, the individual receiving the word must fight in the Spirit, as the promise will sometimes be tested. The night before Peter was to be executed, he was sleeping in prison, knowing that God must come through and free him. He could not die prematurely, as Christ's prophetic promise was that he would die an old man.

Throughout the years, I have known of several ministers who were in the prime of their life and were stricken with a sudden disease. They had to battle for their recovery, by using the written Word of God and speaking out a confession of faith. They also had to remind God and the adversary that they had a specific God-given assignment that had not yet come to pass.

The fact that they knew their work was not finished stirred within them a great determination to defeat the disease and extend their life, so that they could complete their assignment. One minister's life was extended seven years, while the life of another was extended over thirty years after a cancer diagnosis. Both lived to see the promises fulfilled.

Medical doctors have noted that, if a person yields to any disease and loses hope, they will experience declining health and increase their chances of passing away. However, if they believe they have a future and choose to fight for it, many have extended their lives for years.

If you are dealing with a physical struggle, do not allow the adversary to control your thoughts. As a Christian, you win in both life and death. However, determine that you will fulfill your number of days. Be like Paul, knowing that when your departure time has arrived, only then will you say, "Now I am ready. I fought a good fight, I have kept the faith, and now there is laid up for me a crown of righteousness...." (2 Tim. 4:6-8).

CHAPTER 9

A TIME TO DIE AND A TIME NOT TO DIE

Numerous scriptures teach that God promises believers the possibility of a long life. We read:

> *"My son, do not forget my law, But let your heart keep my commands; For length of days and long life and peace they will add to you."*
> —PROV. 3:2

> *"With long life will I satisfy him and show him my salvation."*
> — PSALM 91:16

> *"For by Me your days shall be multiplied, and the years of your life shall be increased."*
> — PROV. 9:11

> *"Honor your father and mother that your days may be long upon the land...."*
> — EXOD. 20:12

These verses and others indicate that God has provided promises for a long life. Abraham died and was buried at a good old age (Gen. 25:8). King Joash died at a good old age (Judg. 8:32). David died at a good old age (1 Chron. 29:28). Abraham lived 175 years (Gen. 25:7),

Isaac lived 180 years (Gen. 35:28), Jacob lived 147 years (Gen. 47:28), and his son Joseph died at 110 years of age (Gen. 50:22).

With sacred scripture indicating that God allows a person in covenant with Him to live a long life that ends at a good old age, why have so many Christians passed way years before the time promised in the Word of God?

King Solomon wrote about the seasons in human life. He said there is "a time to be born and a time to die" (Eccl. 3:2). While meditating on death, he penned an interesting thought in Ecclesiastes 7:17: "Do not be excessively wicked and do not be a fool. Why should you die before your time?" This indicates that it is possible to die before your assigned time.

There is an assumption that if a person dies young or before their seventies, it must have been their time to go. This might not always be the case. Sometimes people attempt to comfort the bereaved with statements such as, "God took her because He needed another angel in heaven," or "God took him because He needed more people in the heavenly choir." These kinds of statements are not only untrue, but they can also cause the grieving individual more distress. God already has two angels for every fallen one, so He doesn't need more angels (Rev. 12:4). God has Satan and his hosts outnumbered. God also doesn't need the earth's best singers, because the heavenly choir will be made up of saints from every tribe and nation (Rev. 5:9).

The possibility of dying before your time can be caused by any number of controllable or uncontrollable circumstances. Consider some of the reasons that people around the world experience an early death.

Disease and sickness can lead to premature death. Some diseases are linked to personal choices—diet, alcohol, smoking, and so on. People in poor nations are susceptible to sickness and disease because they have no control over problems such as famine and unsanitary conditions in the land. In wealthier nations, people have a plethora of choices, but sometimes they choose unwisely.

Too many deaths are caused by illegal drug overdoses. Observe the current crisis in the United States where, in one year, 112,000 people died from fentanyl overdoses alone. This eclipses every previous drug epidemic. A person cannot take a pill from someone and assume that it's a painkiller or antidepressant just because it looks like the real thing. Drug cartels are pressing pills to make them look like a legal pharmaceutical grade drug, when in fact they are laced with deadly substances, including fentanyl. Drug overdoses are a leading cause of death among Americans aged eighteen to forty-five.

Several years ago, a divorced mother and her son moved to Cleveland, Tennessee and began to attend services at our church. The young man, a believer, enrolled at a local Christian university, worked part time at a local restaurant, and eventually served on the church prayer team. He felt that he was called to be a missionary and kept a globe on his dresser, praying about where God might want to send him. Jacob was a kind, friendly, and responsible young man, and you rarely saw him without a smile on his face.

Jacob began to have pain from his wisdom teeth, and a dentist recommended they be removed. The dentist prescribed pain medication during this time, and unfortunately, Jacob became addicted to it. When he ran out of the prescription painkiller, he started buying and taking Xanax.

His behavior began to change, and eventually his life spiraled out of control. There was one challenge after another, which led to the young man spending time in drug rehabilitation. When he was off drugs, things were great and life returned to normal. But like a roller coaster, he would come off the drug, get his life back on the right track, and then without warning succumb to the drug temptation again. People who knew this young man, even law enforcement, liked him and recognized his potential. Nobody wanted to see him throw away his life with drugs.

One Christmas morning, he and his mother had a heated conversation about drugs. She noticed that his behavior was changing again, but he didn't want to be forced to leave home, nor did he want to return to rehab. He wanted his testimony to be that God instantly delivered and set him free from drugs. He expressed his desire to get radical about his faith again and stop wasting time on things that weren't important. That night they watched movies together and had an enjoyable conversation.

The next morning, his mother went to his room to wake him up for breakfast. She soon realized he was not breathing and called 911. His death was ruled an accidental overdose; he had taken what he thought was Xanax, but it was laced with fentanyl.

Sad stories like this are repeated over and over, as an addiction takes control of someone's life and destroys everything God had planned for their future.

Paul the apostle wrote in 1 Corinthians 3:16-17:

> *"Know ye not that ye are the temple of God, and that the Spirit of God dwells in you? If any man defile the temple of God, him shall God destroy; for the temple of God is holy, which temple are ye."*

In this verse, he compared our physical body to the temple of God and told us not to defile ourselves or else we will be destroyed. The Greek word for defile is *phtheirei*, meaning *to corrupt, spoil, destroy, ruin, shrivel or wither away*. Something that defiles will impact the body in a dangerous or negative manner. If you do things that inflict negative consequences on your body, this verse implies that God will not *prevent* physical destruction from overtaking you. By willfully defiling your body, you are agreeing to your own destruction.

An untold number of deaths are caused by global wars, terrorism, gang wars, drug cartels, and evil government leaders. Many innocent people become their victims.

Nearly every country on earth has dealt with deaths caused by natural disasters—hurricanes, earthquakes, tsunamis, flooding, droughts, or tornados. Every year, approximately forty thousand to fifty thousand people die globally from such disasters.

In the United States alone, over a quarter million people die every year from unintentional deaths. These could be a result of tragedies such as automobile and motorcycle accidents, falls, workplace accidents, and accidents in the home.

When my wife and I were traveling on a winding two-lane West Virginia road last year, a motorcycle driver rounded a curve and crossed the line, lost control, and was headed straight for our car. I had prayed that morning because I felt a burden for someone on the highway that day. The motorcycle slid across the road and stopped within inches of our car. Thankfully, the driver seemed to be okay, but incidents such as this don't always have a positive outcome.

The accident that took the life of my beloved cousin Louanna was caused by an eighty-year-old man who was hauling cattle and decided to run a red light as he sped down a hill. The driver of the first car through the green light watched in horror as the truck slammed into the driver's door of Louanna's car and pushed her over seventy-five feet. The first car was in the right place to avoid being hit. Louanna was in the wrong place at exactly the wrong time.

Unintentional deaths can be caused by someone else's faulty work. Vehicles and airplanes can have design flaws that cause tragic accidents and deaths. Mechanics can make human errors that result in deaths.

All but three states in the United States have experienced an increase in homicides, which are higher now than at any time in recorded history. Sometimes the victims are simply in the wrong place at the wrong time. Sometimes they are involved with the wrong people.

Many people live to be a good old age and simply pass away because it is their time to go. But a countless number of people are taken from us in sudden and unexpected ways, and many die through no fault of their own.

THE "god" OF THIS WORLD

The Bible tells us that Satan is "the god of this world, who has blinded the eyes of those who do not believe" (2 Cor. 4:4). Satan also has limited authority to attempt to politically dominate world kingdoms. Satan informed Jesus that he was given the kingdoms of the world and could give them to whomever he willed (Luke 4:6). Satan is also called "the prince of this world" (John 12:31; 14:30).

Christ spoke of Satan having his own kingdom (Matt. 12:26), and Paul revealed that Satan's hierarchy is ranked in four levels—principalities, powers, the rulers of the darkness of this world, and spiritual wickedness in high places (Eph. 6:12). Christ showed John in Revelation that the dragon (a symbol for Satan) has power, a throne, and authority, which he transfers to the Antichrist during the time of the tribulation (Rev. 13:2).

Satan works behind the scenes in many world governments, large cities, and even small towns, raising up unrighteous leaders by blinding people spiritually and dulling their understanding and hearing. Sinners are motivated toward unrighteousness, including criminal enterprises, theft, murder, and other dangerous activities. This is the reality of the world in which we live. People around the world suffer from the rule of tyrannical leaders and evildoers who indiscriminately take innocent lives. The goal of Satan is to kill, steal, and destroy (John 10:10), and he uses willing human vessels to accomplish his demonic purposes.

The enemy still has his limitations. In the book of Job, Satan could steal Job's animals and create a storm that caused the roof of the house to collapse and kill his ten children. Job was afflicted with painful boils. However, God put a leash on Satan and told him that he was not permitted to take Job's life (Job 2:6). God allowed the attack, but Satan instigated it. In the end, there was a divine reversal, and Job received double for his trouble (Job 42:10).

Each day, death stalks the globe and snatches the rich and the poor, the great and the small, the free and the bound. Death does not respect our established boundaries.

One day in the future, Christ and God the Father will take control and put all His enemies under His feet. The last enemy that will be destroyed is death (1 Cor. 15:24-26). Until that time, there will be some things we simply cannot control. As long as so much of the world is dominated by Satan's influence, *bad things will happen to good people because of bad people.*

Solomon wrote that being overly wicked is a path to dying before your time. He told us that there is "a time to be born and a time to die" (Eccl. 3:2). Paul called death an "appointment" (Heb. 9:27). There are many ways in which to die before your time, but one way to fulfill your full number of days is by walking in obedience to God and following His spiritual laws.

What if I were to ask, "Are you one hundred percent sure that your sins are forgiven and you are born again and a follower of Christ? And when you die, do you know that you will be escorted by angels into paradise in heaven?" If you would immediately holler out, "I know I'm ready to go," then you have expressed confidence in your faith and in Christ. If you must pause and think about it, or if you would say, "I'm not sure," then you might not be ready. Your conscience has already judged you, and your lack of confession has exposed you. Receive Christ, repent, change your behavior, and know where you are going. Then stay on that narrow road until the end.

IN LOVING MEMORY
OF OUR FAMILY & FRIENDS

Louanna Bava Carr, 1960 – 2024

Fred Stone prior to his departure.

Allison Kile, passed at age 39 on Feb. 6, 2004

Jacob Krummert, 23, passed on Christmas Day

Andrew Ridpath, passed 2005 at age 20

Tracy Davis, passed age 25, Pam's close friend

Best "Cuz" Ever

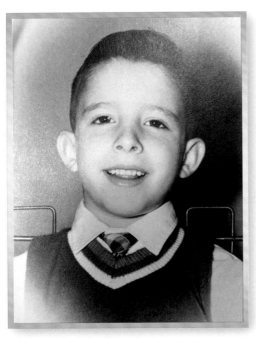

Perry Age 9

Louanna Age 9

Fred and Perry

Louanna and her father, Joe Bava

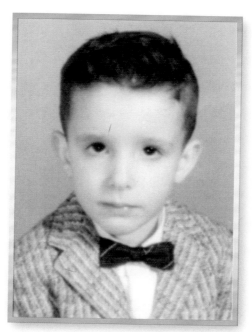

Perry age 4

Perry and his sister Diana, Christmas 1960

Parsons, West Virginia

Dr Michael in Parsons who delivered both of us

Parsons Hospital where Perry and Louanna were born 18 months apart

MEMORIES OF FAMILY

Grandad and Grandma Bava, Louanna and Perry at Millie's House August 1996

Some of the Bava Family

My sweet Italian family at Uncle Joe's funeral

Family Memories

Lu -Lu, the family comedian, with me and Dad

Cousin Connie, Aunt Norma, Dad, and Louanna at Elkins West Virginia

More Memories
From Our Albums

Cousins, Aunts, Mom and Dad

Joe Bava Jr. and his sister Louanna

Coach Bava, she played
basketball in school

Aunt Millie's house eating spaghetti

Cousins Connie, Lu and Diane

Aunt Janet, Louanna, Perry, and cousin Steve

Aunt Janet and Louanna at my revival

Louanna and Pam, April 2024

Headed to church in a new outfit

One of our last pictures at conference

Louanna and Johanna Stone

Louanna's Nieces - Perry's third cousins

Louanna and her sister Connie headed to church

Louanna and her sweet husband Pat Carr

Shweiki, Perry, Louanna and Pam before conference

They bring cookies to their diabetic cousin!

Four great people - Connie, Louanna, Pam, and Aunt Janet

She was always smiling

Taken in Elkins, West Virginia after the "treasure" was discovered

January 2024 - My last trip from Pat and Louanna's house

Cousins Billy Bennett and Louanna searching Aunt Millie's house with Perry

All my cousins from Uncle Joe Bava's family

Give the bill to Louanna!

Ready for church

Christmas time is always a big
family celebration.

Football in the fall. Our favorite time.

My West Virginia bucket list trip, October 2023

Our Last Picture with my sister Diana and Louanna
April 25 2024

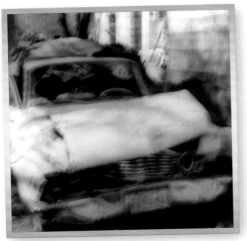

Perry's accident, near Elkin's, West Virginia around 1962-63

Louanna's accident, near Elkin's, West Virginia May 25, 12:35 2024

WE WILL ALWAYS REMEMBER YOU AND CAN'T WAIT TO SEE YOU AGAIN!

CHAPTER 10

I NEED TO KNOW WHY, BUT GOD IS SILENT

After most tragedies there are always more questions than answers. Why would a healthy person in the best years of life, someone who still has goals and plans for the future, someone who still anticipates years of enjoyment ahead with family and friends, be taken from us?

Asking yourself why can control your thinking every waking moment. Years ago, my dear friend, Pastor Walter Hallum, experienced the tragedy of his seventeen-year-old daughter dying in a plane crash. God spoke to him to be cautious about allowing grief to overtake him. It is quite normal to mourn and experience weeks or months of sorrow when someone you love is taken from you. However, grief can become a spiritual stronghold that grips the heart and paralyzes the life of the sufferer.

When a ninety-year-old passes away, we don't ask why, since death is expected once we reach a certain age. When a thirty-year-old departs this life, we expected them to live another half century or longer. Babies are expected to grow up and outlive their parents. When the expected becomes the unexpected, we ask why. Often, we are left with questions we cannot answer.

THE ENDLESS WHY

Job was a businessman who was considered the greatest in the east. He was upright, blameless, feared God, and shunned evil (Job 1:1-3). He offered burnt offerings on behalf of his children, just in case they had sinned or cursed God. It might have been impossible to find a man more undeserving of all the trouble the enemy brought into his life.

In today's economy, Job's land, homes, animals, and possessions might be valued at tens of millions of dollars. Once Satan was given permission to attack, all at once a great wind caused the house to crash down upon his ten children, killing all of them. A lighting strike consumed seven thousand sheep and some of the servants. Two nomadic tribes, the Sabeans and the Chaldeans, raided the land and stole the oxen, donkeys, and camels. They killed all but one servant who escaped to tell Job what transpired.

A second wave of trouble struck Job when he was afflicted with boils from head to toe. Even after all that, Job never blamed God for his crisis. He told his wife, "Shall we indeed accept good from God and not accept adversity?" Through it all, Job did not sin, nor did he blame God (Job 1:22).

The King James translation says that Job did not charge God foolishly. We think of the word charge as a legal term to indicate that a person has been found guilty of a crime. Job never treated God as some criminal who stole, killed, and destroyed. Instead, Job said, "Naked I came from my mother's womb, and naked shall I return there. The LORD gave, and the LORD has taken away; Blessed be the name of the LORD" (Job 1:21).

However, his grief was so great that three of his closest friends arrived and sat with him to "comfort him." For seven days and nights, nothing was spoken. Job was so heartbroken he could not speak, and none of his friends spoke, either (Job 3:13).

The friends' empathy turned to judgmental reasoning when they attempted to explain *why* the trouble came. Later, God spoke and revealed that all three friends were wrong in their opinion editorials. The attack was from Satan; it was an attempt to weaken Job's faith and cause him to curse God for his crisis (Job 1:11; 2:5,9).

Despite Job's trust in God, the *why* question remained. Throughout the entire book of Job, fourteen times he questioned why. In Job 3:11, he even questioned, "Why did I not die at birth? Why did I not perish when I came from the womb? He explains that, had he died at birth, he would have been at rest in death (Job 3:13).

ASKING WHY

David's life can seem like an enigma. He was a man after God's own heart, yet at times he struggled with his carnal nature and made some terrible choices. His sins temporarily stole his mental peace and joy of the Lord. David endured many sleepless nights as he cried out to God and petitioned Him for help. Reading the Psalms, we get an idea of how many times David asked why:

- Psalm 22:1 — Why have you forsaken me?

- Psalm 42:9 — Why have you forgotten me?

- Psalm 42:11 — Why is my soul cast down?

- Psalm 74:11 — Why is your right hand withdrawn from me?

- Psalm 80:12 — Why is the hedge broken down?

The odd fact is that David knew why. It was his sin. David understood that his crisis was self-invited, yet he still asked why. He had engaged in adultery with a married woman, gotten her pregnant, then attempted to set up the husband to have relations with her to cover the sin. When this didn't work, David arranged to have the husband killed in battle.

The child died soon after birth. David's sin was made public, and some of his friends turned against him. He could not sleep, and later suffered from a physical disease (Psa. 38:7-10).

However, David refused to blame God for any of this. Before his child died, David fasted and prayed for one week for the child's healing. After the child died, he arose, washed himself, and worshipped God. He took his chastisement from God, humbled himself, and never gave up (2 Samuel 12).

When an unexpected death comes, it is normal to ask God why this happened. However, follow the examples of Job and David, and be careful to avoid blaming God.

On the evening of February 11, 1977, well-known evangelist Oral Roberts lost his thirty-seven-year-old daughter, Rebecca Nash, and her husband, Marshall. They were returning home from a ski trip when they, three other passengers, and the pilot were killed in a terrible plane crash that happened during a rainstorm. The plane disintegrated nine thousand feet in the air and spewed wreckage over a mile and a half of farmland. Some argued that the accident was pilot error, and others said the plane's automatic pilot malfunctioned and caused further problems with the aircraft.

Having experienced the death of a daughter, Oral Roberts contacted Walter Hallum after his daughter was killed in a plane crash to tell him that after his own daughter was killed, the Lord impressed upon him not to start asking why. If he did, he would be asking this the rest of his life. The Lord told Oral, "There are things about this you will never know until you get to heaven."

WHEN THE RIGHTEOUS ARE TAKEN

There is a scripture in the Old Testament that I have noted when friends or family suddenly passed away. I was quickened to this verse shortly after my mother died. It is Isaiah 57:1 and it speaks to the taking of the righteous.

Years ago, a pastor friend with two teenaged sons had to deal with an unexpected tragedy. After a Sunday night service, one of his sons, who was about sixteen at the time, left the church with his girlfriend to go out and eat with the youth from the church. Soon sirens were heard as police and an ambulance sped down the road. Another driver had crossed the line and hit the son's vehicle head on. His car was so mangled that the response team did not immediately know that two people were in the car. His body had been thrown under the dash and was rolled up.

The pastor was under unbearable grief, questioning why this happened and why God did not intervene. The struggle persisted for months, but no answer came. One day he felt impressed to read from the Bible, and that is when he came across this verse. For him, it gave a possible explanation for *why* this could have happened:

> *"The righteous perishes, and no man takes it to heart; merciful men are taken away, while no one considers that the righteous is taken away from evil"* [to come].
>
> – ISAIAH 57:1 (NKJV)

This verse could explain, in some situations, an answer to the question, *Why do righteous people pass away young or unexpectedly?* Sometimes the righteous are taken from the evil to come. In the case of the pastor, years later he sensed that, had his son lived, he could have strayed from the Lord and lived in a backslidden spiritual condition. At the time of his death, the young man was living a Christian life and was ready to meet the Lord. However, had the boy grown up and turned his back on God, he could have died in a lifestyle of unrepentant sin and stepped into eternal darkness.

In 2021, my mother was diagnosed with covid pneumonia and experienced breathing difficulties. She was admitted to the local hospital and, after twelve days, seemed to be on the verge of recovering. Then we received a call one night during a church service that her heart had stopped. Nurses spent ten minutes reviving her, but they told us that if we wanted to see her, we should come now. For the first time since she was hospitalized, we were allowed to stand by her bedside. She was unable to communicate in any manner, and she passed away shortly after we arrived.

I wondered why she was getting better, and then suddenly she died. She was eighty-five years old, but she still had a strong mind and still drove to our office to work every day. As time passed and I thought about it, I was somewhat relieved for her.

First, Dad had passed away ten years earlier, and she missed him. She had some physical problems that caused her constant pain. She fell a couple of times, and one time the fall caused a broken wrist and ankle that required surgery and landed her in a nursing and rehabilitation facility for three months. She was concerned about expensive repairs needed on the house, and there were other things that weighed on her mind. And while she had always been active, she knew that she was slowing down, and it would become harder for her to do the things she enjoyed. She never would have wanted to be in a long-term care facility. Had she not gotten sick, she might have lived into her nineties, but perhaps not with the quality of life she desired.

I knew that she was in heaven, and I was glad that she had no more physical suffering. There were other negative situations which her death kept her from having to be concerned about. I believe God spared her from the negative situations by permitting her to pass on to the next life.

WATCH YOUR WORDS

Many Christians are concerned about the spiritual condition of their loved ones, and sometimes they become so frustrated that they pray, "*Whatever it takes*, I want them saved." My cousin Louanna was concerned about everyone in the family making it to heaven. She mentioned one particular person and said, "I have prayed that whatever it takes to get his attention and know that he's saved, that it will happen." Sometimes she would confess that, even if something had to happen to her to get his attention, she was ready for it.

I understand the burden she was under, as this person was up in years and had a potentially serious physical condition. At the same time, her words bothered me, because so many times when someone prays "whatever it takes," a tragic event occurs. This confession could remove a hedge and permit a crisis or tragedy that might be exceedingly difficult to deal with.

Nevertheless, we have all seen people come to Christ after a crisis, and especially after the death of a loved one. God has put eternity in our hearts, and such events often stir up the conviction of the Holy Spirit, causing a sinner to realize their need for a Savior. However, before saying, "whatever it takes," be ready for something that might not be a pleasant experience.

The words we speak will release life or death, both for ourselves and for others. Guard your conversation, as consistent negativity could shorten your days or someone else's. Wrong words that opened the door to sickness, oppression, and fear could be one reason why some have died before their time.

ABIDING IN REBELLION

Psalm 55:23 reads, "But thou, O God, shalt bring them down into the pit of destruction: bloody and deceitful men shall not live out half their days; but I will trust in thee."

In Hebrew, a "bloody man" is a violent person who sheds the blood of others. We would call this person a murderer.

The first sin that infected the universe was pride that led to rebellion. It happened when Satan initiated a conspiracy against God and was cast out of heaven. God noted that rebellion is as the sin of witchcraft (1 Samuel 15:23). Proverbs 29:1 tells us, "He who is often rebuked, and hardens his neck, will suddenly be destroyed, and that without remedy."

The word rebuke is a correction that is meant to lead someone to change their direction. The New Testament word is *conviction*, which can also be the English word reprove, used in John 16:8. This word means to convict, to rebuke, and to tell a fault. In this case the Holy Spirit is revealing a sin or a fault and pressing people to turn away from their trespasses.

Notice in Proverbs 29:1 that the phrase is "often rebuked." For a hundred years, God attempted to turn Noah's generation toward Him. Only eight souls listened. God warned, "My Spirit will not always strive (deal) with man" (Gen. 6:3).

The Proverbs warning reveals the *resistance* of the person or persons God is dealing with. The Israelites rebelled against God and were called "stiff-necked." The Hebrew term means a neck that will not turn and only looks in one direction—the wrong one. A stiff-necked person closes their ears and refuses to listen. The person who persists has the potential of being "suddenly destroyed and without remedy." This speaks of breaking something into pieces. The idea of "no remedy," would mean with no solution. It is something that happens and there is no way out.

NOT WHY, BUT WHERE

We all will have a time when we ask why. However, for those who are still alive, the most important question is *where*?

Where will you spend eternity after you breathe your final breath on your last day on earth? There could be many *whys*, but there is only one *where*. You have two choices for where you will spend eternity—heaven or hell—and you will spend it at one of those two places. You will either spend eternity with God, or eternity separated from God. Why is a temporary question. Where is a permanent location. *Where lasts forever.*

CHAPTER 11

SEASONS OF A
BROKEN HEART

Contrary to what we might think, the phrase "a broken heart" is not simply a metaphor to describe how we feel when something terrible happens. Medically, a broken heart does not refer to the heart literally splitting in half, but there is a condition the medical community refers to as "broken heart syndrome."

Rare but serious, it can cause heart attack-like symptoms in response to a severe emotional or physical event. We often hear this expression after someone has passed away unexpectedly, or after the loss of a lifelong companion. Symptoms can begin within minutes or hours of any highly stressful or traumatic event. The heart muscle suddenly becomes weakened, or it can fail altogether. In rare cases this condition can be fatal. However, most people recover from a broken heart within a few months.

I know of a situation where a woman lost both of her sons in automobile accidents, and then her husband passed away. The woman was consumed with such grief that she lay in bed all day and would get up only to go to the restroom or the kitchen. She had no appetite and never went outside. The grief had permanently set up residence in her mind and spirit to the point that she was emotionally paralyzed.

When a person has no joy, won't go outside, and loses all desire to live, this causes people to believe there's nothing to look forward to. This type of grief leads to isolation and separation from people, and it makes the situation even worse.

The death of someone you love will produce two human emotions: *grief* and *sorrow*. The New Testament Greek word for sorrow is *lupe*, and it refers to a *heavy feeling of sadness*. If allowed to persist too long, sadness develops into despair and depression. Most people seldom experience despair because we understand that negative circumstances can be altered, and things will eventually turn out for our good.

Death is different, though. If the deceased was a believer, there is hope and peace in knowing that we will see the person again. Still, the thought of never again seeing or talking to them on earth, never hugging them, never watching them grow up and have a family, and having an empty chair at the dinner table is painful.

While sorrow is a common emotion, *grief* is part of the death process. Grief creates a sense of anxiety. If we continually carry grief, it will make a person physically and emotionally sick. It will cause us to lose all desire for fellowship with others, lose our appetite, and lose sleep. Don't let grief become your constant companion.

EXPECTED AND UNEXPECTED DEPARTURES

Sometimes we aren't surprised by someone's death because we expected it. Other times, death is a complete shock because it was so sudden and unanticipated.

In the late 1980s, Pam received a call that her best friend, Tracy Davis, had been killed in a car accident near Birmingham, Alabama. Tracy loved Pam like a sister. Our son Jonathan had been born and Tracy spoke of moving to Cleveland to be a nanny for Jonathan. Eyewitnesses to the accident said there was a girl driving and a man in the passenger's seat, yet Tracy was driving alone in the car. Pam and I believe it was an angel coming to receive her spirit.

My dad passed away at age seventy-eight after being hospitalized and then admitted to a local care facility. Dad was ready to go be with Jesus and had felt for several months that his organs were shutting down. We knew that without a miracle, Dad would soon leave us.

My mother had been doing well until she contracted covid-19 and was hospitalized in the intensive care unit. Like so many who died after being hospitalized for covid, the protocol was deadlier than the disease and she passed away from a heart attack. She was eighty-five years of age.

One of the hardest deaths was my beloved grandfather, John Bava. He was a multi-talented man who had been a coal miner, pastor, musician, singer, songwriter, author, publisher, and builder. He could keep people in stitches laughing, and he was one of the jolliest people I ever knew. I loved being around him. I was ministering in Africa when he was admitted to the hospital for emergency surgery. He had a couple of strokes while in the hospital, and the neurologist claimed he was brain dead. We knew better, because he was able to let us know he heard us, even though they had him heavily sedated and on oxygen. I flew back from Africa and was able to see him before he left this life. He was eighty-four.

My grandmother, Lucy Bava, spent five years grieving the loss of Granddad. She was diagnosed with pancreatic cancer and lived to be eighty-six, taking her journey to heaven from a Cleveland hospital.

The year before Grandad died, he had begun to dream about his family members who were in heaven. They were beckoning him to come home. The day before Grandmother died, she dreamed of seeing my grandfather in heaven, and he showed her the massive banquet hall where the Marriage Supper of the Lamb would take place. He told her, "We are getting things ready now."

Joe Bava, the father of my cousin Louanna, died almost exactly a year after his brother John, my grandfather. Our precious family members were between seventy-eight and eighty-six years of age when they crossed the finish line of their race (Heb. 12:1-2). Even though they lived to a good old age and we knew they went to heaven, the family still felt sorrow and grief when they left us. We missed them, and the sense of loss persisted for a long time.

There was a *different kind of sorrow and grief* when my precious cousin Louanna passed. It was a level that I had not experienced with my older relatives. I asked myself why. Why was this death so difficult?

When I am asked questions, I am expected to reply with some kind of answer. When I have questions, I go to the Bible and research the Word until I find an answer. In reply to the question of why some deaths are more difficult, I believe there are four possible answers to which a grieving individual can relate.

1. The Death was Sudden and Unexpected

When family or friends are mature in age, or when they have lived with a long term debilitating or terminal disease, we know that without a supernatural miracle from God, the angel of death will eventually pay a visit to their bedside. We have time to prepare emotionally, with the knowledge that everybody has an appointment with death.

However, it is different when someone is in perfect health, excited about their future, and expected to have many years ahead of them. When we hear that they are gone, the shock of loss and separation sets in immediately and can last a long time.

When a spouse or a child doesn't wake up in the morning, or when someone unexpectedly drops to the floor and cannot be revived, the survivors experience a sudden and high level of distress. There was no chance to say goodbye. All the plans they've made are gone in the wind. Children are left without a parent. The income they provided is suddenly gone. Not only must people deal with the shock of the death, but they also are forced to make plans for how they will live without this person going forward.

Louanna and our family had some big plans. She was planning to go to Israel with us. She had not yet eaten at my favorite restaurant in Gatlinburg. We were discussing a big family trip to our great-granddad Pete's hometown in Calabria, Italy. Our Aunt Millie had a cedar chest at her house that was locked, and nobody could find the key. We were like searchers on a treasure hunt, wondering what Millie concealed in the trunk years ago and how we were going to get into it without a key. We were hoping to open it together with our cousin Billy as we continued our search for historic family items.

The day that Louanna died, all those plans vanished, along with the memories we never had a chance to make. Clearly, a sudden and unexpected death brings a different level of sorrow and grief. I refer to this emotion as "sudden sorrow."

Contrast that with the death of someone like my dad. When he was admitted to the nursing facility, I was able to spend a few nights with him, just the two of us. I talked to him and prayed for him. He knew what I was saying, but he was in no condition to talk. At times I prayed audibly past midnight. It was an unforgettable memory. He would soon transition to heaven, and we all knew it. You can emotionally prepare when you understand that death is approaching.

2. The Attachment of a Bloodline

Most people who share a family bloodline have a level of closeness and relationship that they will never have with non-family members. The sharing of common ancestors and decades of history creates a solid bond between relatives. This might be more evident among people of certain cultures, such as Italians and Hispanics, who are known to be close and family oriented.

We can be close to our spiritual family, but they are not our biological family. It is simply not the same. With my cousin, we knew each other growing up, and she financially supported the ministry for years. We knew the same people and the same places, and she knew some crazy family stories that I had never heard.

The family link creates a non-judgmental safe place where people can be loved because they're family. Even when they're upset with you, arguing with you about something, or grumbling about you to another family member, your biological family still loves you unconditionally. People outside your biological family might like you today and despise you tomorrow. It's rare to find non-biological people, including in the church, who love you the way your family loves you. Losing someone like this puts a hole in your heart, as their absence creates a large void.

3. The Level of Love

At the time of the writing of the New Testament, the Greeks had four words used to describe love: agape, phileo, storge, and eros.

Agape is the word used to describe the love that God has for humanity. This is the highest form of love, a perfect love, which expresses God's very nature: God *is* love. God manifested agape love by giving us the ultimate gift of Jesus Christ, who came to reconcile sinners back to God. He loved us, so we ought to love one another (1 John 4:7-12; John 3:16).

In his book, *Sparkling Gems from the Greek*, scholar Rick Renner says that agape is a baffling word for translators because it is filled with so much deep meaning and emotion. This is how Rick clarified the meaning of the word:

> *"Agape occurs when an individual sees, recognizes, understands, or appreciates the value of an object or a person, causing the viewer to behold this object or person in great esteem, awe, admiration, wonder, and sincere appreciation. Such great respect is awakened in the heart of the observer for the object or*

person he is beholding that he is compelled to love it." (Sparkling Gems from the Greek, page 525)

Agape love extends mercy, grace, and forgiveness; it is sacrificial, giving love that seeks to do good to all. If you are blessed to have an agape friend, this friend will love you always and for life.

Philia love is a brotherly-sisterly love that shows affection and kindness toward others, and it has the connotation of close friendship. Variations of the word also refer to hospitality.

Philia is used in Romans 12:10 where Paul wrote, "Be kindly affectionate to one another with *brotherly love*, in honor giving preference to one another." First Peter 3:8-9 tells us to have compassion for one another, love as brothers, be tenderhearted, be courteous, do not return evil for evil or reviling for reviling, and be a blessing so that you may inherit a blessing. Verse seven instructs husbands to show this same kind of love and courtesy to their wives.

Stergo is a Greek word that describes the love between family members, especially parents and children. Families have a different kind of love that develops because of the bond of familiarity, dependence, devotion, values, and traditions. Stergo love creates an unbreakable bond which lasts for a lifetime.

Regrettably, some people never had a chance to experience this kind of familial love. Family life for some people was one traumatic event after another that led to nothing but a lifetime of scars.

Second Timothy 3:2-3 warns us of perilous times that will come in the last days. People will be lovers of self, lovers of money, lovers of pleasure, disobedient to parents, and unloving. The love of self, money, and pleasure leads to the breakdown of families, traditions, and values.

We see the potential for this kind of breakdown in the definition of another Greek word for love: *eros*. This is the Greek term used for physical love and sexual desire, and from it we get the word erotic. Eros seeks to gratify desires of the flesh. Outside the covenant of marriage, eros is defined as a low level of love that is self-seeking and self-serving.

People who focus only on themselves have a difficult time showing agape, philia, or stergo love to others, or even giving honor, appreciation, mercy, and forgiveness to others. The Bible teaches us to love God and love others. Jesus was asked, "What is the greatest commandment in the law?" He replied:

> "You shall love the LORD your God with all your heart, with all your soul, and with all your mind. This is the first and great commandment. And the second is like it: 'You shall love your neighbor as yourself.'
>
> – MATTHEW 22:37-39 (NKJV)

Examining the distinct kinds of love helps us see why we are drawn to some people more than others. It helps us understand why we have a different kind of love for our own family.

Developing love for someone—even love for God—is built upon *knowing* a person and having a *relationship* with them. The meaning of the word relationship has changed over the decades, but centuries ago the word meant, "sense or state of being related by kindred, affinity, or other alliance." We *relate* to build a *relationship*. Best friends connect because they relate to one another. Christians choose a specific church because they align with the church's doctrinal beliefs and because they develop relationships and form bonds of brotherly and sisterly love with other church members. For some, it is the bonds of *philia love* that pull them back like a magnet, service after service.

It can be difficult for unbelievers to grasp the agape love of God. They might not understand the simple phrase, "Jesus loves and cares about you," if their whole life is a continual crisis and they have no *relationship* with Christ. Sinners have difficulty relating to a God they have never seen or heard, do not know, and have never learned much about.

Once a sinner repents, they begin to engage in communication (prayer) and worship to God, along with fellowship with other Christians. They are taught to read the Bible regularly and grow in faith. These actions unlock a sense of deep love and affection between God and the seeker. The difference is that now they have entered a relationship. The love they experience is built upon the foundation of relationship.

Love is a meaningless word when it is spoken from the mouth but not from the heart. It is easy to speak Christianese language with the mouth and not from the heart as we say to other people, "I love you brother (or sister)." Yet we might have little to no relationship or fellowship with them. We can appreciate people and be thankful for them, and as Christians, we should love a person in the love of the Lord. However, you develop the deepest love for people when you have experienced three ships: *fellowship, friendship*, and an uplifting *relationship*.

Proverbs 18:24 teaches, "A man that hath *friends* must show himself *friendly*: there is a *friend* that sticks closer than a brother." In this passage there are two different Hebrew words for friend. The first word is *rea* and is the Hebrew word for a companion or a close associate. To show yourself friendly means the relationship is reciprocal—you also are a companion or close associate.

The second Hebrew word is *ahab*, which refers to someone with whom you have shared affection. This could be a close friendship or a familial relationship, such as a husband and wife being best friends, or a close relationship with other relatives. It can speak to covenant loyalty. The Proverbs verse clearly tells us that we can have a friend who sticks closer than any familial brother. This is good news for anybody who didn't experience stergo love within their own biological family.

Ahab friends will share one another's burdens and rejoice when their friend rejoices. *Ahab* friends cry when the other cries; they share their pain and losses.

The level of love in a friendship or relationship helps explain why the death of some people in our lives causes so much sorrow and grief. Even as a young child, I deeply loved my Granddad Bava. He was regularly upset with me for changing all the settings on his audio equipment; but even in that, he had a profound influence on my life. It was emotionally difficult to see him go.

My cousin Louanna reminded me so much of Granddad Bava. He told interesting stories, told jokes everywhere he went, and smiled more than anyone I knew. He was a sincerely jolly man. Louanna was the same—always smiling, laughing, and joking.

It is easier to deal with the deaths of people with whom we do not have a strong relationship, even though we might have loved that person. When our brothers and sisters in Christ are taken from us, we likely loved them with a *philia* love. Your strongest level of sorrow and grief, however, is reserved for the people with whom you had the deepest love and relationship—a child, a marital companion, a close relative, or a lifelong friend and confidant.

4. The Level of a Trusted Friend

Jesus spoke of three types of people: *hirelings, servants,* and *friends.* He taught that the third level—that of a friend—is different, because a friend is permitted to know things that others are not. He said:

> *"No longer do I call you servants, for a servant does not know what his master is doing; but I have called you friends, for all things that I heard from My Father I have made known to you."*
>
> – JOHN 15:15

Many people are too carnally minded, selfish, or simply incapable of being a trusted friend. Consider it a blessing if you have a few trusted friends. When you find one, losing them to death brings great sorrow.

Most of us have been *hurt and burnt* by people we trusted, especially once they become upset with us or offended about something. I have heard people say, "I love you, brother," and later felt their dagger stabbing me in the back. If you have experienced this, you are not alone.

When we carry emotional wounds, many of which were caused by people thought to be trustworthy, we tend to lock the doors of our heart and become less trusting of everybody. We all need someone in our lives whom we can trust, and for some, that one and only person is Jesus.

Everybody needs a trusted friend with whom they can share personal information, because there are times in life when people just need to talk things out with someone. People need to tell their battle stories and talk about warfare they're encountering. A trusted friend will let you vent, and they know when to listen and how to respond. People also need to know that the things they're sharing will not be blabbed far and wide the moment they close the front door.

According to John 2:23-25, even when people believed in His name and observed the signs He was doing, Jesus would not entrust Himself to them because He knew what was in man. As multitudes gathered to hear His sermons or receive healing, He was their spiritual hero. Yet, after His illegal arrest, He became their archenemy. His own eleven remaining disciples, apart from John, fled the execution scene and chose protection behind locked doors and windows.

It is difficult to lose your best friend, talking pal, and confidant, whether it's a spouse, relative, or a close friend you were blessed to have in your life. The loss feels like a piece of your heart took wings and flew away. When death takes someone whom you trust, someone who cannot easily be replaced, the pain persists for a long time.

THE COMFORT OF THE LORD

In Isaiah 40:1, God instructed the prophet to comfort His people. The verse reads, "Comfort, O comfort My people, says your God." The Hebrew word *comfort* means, "to give breath," or "to give breath again." The death of someone dear to you seems to take the breath from you. Someone described this kind of death as "knocking the breath out of them." Those experiencing such sorrow or grief need comfort.

When God breathed the breath of life into Adam's nostrils, God's own breath caused Adam to become "a living soul" (Gen. 2:7 KJV). Within every living human being is a soul and spirit. Our soul is the breath of God—the *breath of life*—that causes us to have life in a physical body (Job 33:4). At death, the body returns to dust, but the soul and spirit continue to live eternally outside the body. This is why Paul wrote, "to be absent from the body is to be present with the Lord" (2 Cor. 5:8).

Death causes the soul and spirit to be released and to be absent from the mortal body. The Greek word for absent, *ekdemeo*, is from two words meaning *out of* and *the public* or *the people*. Death removes the deceased from public view, away from the people. At the death of a born-again believer in Christ, the soul and spirit enter paradise (2 Cor. 12:2-4). The Greek word that Paul used for *present* with the Lord means, "to be in one's own country; to be home." At death, we leave our earthly home and enter our eternal home.

This agrees with Hebrews 11:13-16 which says that we are strangers and pilgrims on earth who are seeking a homeland in a better country, in a city that God has prepared. Those who transfer from earth to heaven will immediately cease from their labors and enter into rest (see Heb. 4). The dead in Christ are now awaiting their resurrection in a heavenly paradise, a land of beauty and perfection. They are now comforted.

Those remaining on earth also need comfort that permeates their soul. This is not the comfort of kind words such as, "We are praying for you." They need a supernatural peace from the Holy Spirit, whom Jesus called the comforter (John 16:7).

Jesus said that He would not leave us *comfortless* (John 14:18). The Greek word is *orphanos*, meaning an *orphan* without a father or mother. The death of a dear loved one causes an empty feeling, a void in our soul that leaves us brokenhearted. It is the Holy Spirit that reminds us that we are not *orphaned* when tragedy strikes. God can and will comfort us and provide seasons of recovery for the body, mind, and spirit.

Psalm 147:3 reminds us, "He heals the brokenhearted and binds up their wounds." Our greatest comfort is the hope of the resurrection of the dead in Christ. Without this resurrection hope, we of all people are most miserable (1 Cor. 15:19). This is the greatest promise that releases peace to those who remain on earth when they suffer a loss. For believers, one day we will see them, hug them, and fellowship with them again in heaven. We will be with them throughout the thousand-year reign of Christ, and we will live with them on the new earth (Rev. 20-22).

If you are not a believer and you are not following Christ, as long as you are breathing, you still have time to change your path and your final destination. It is a heartbreaking moment to watch parents and siblings stand at the graveside of a family member, knowing the way the deceased lived and died, and with great pain have to question where the soul and spirit of their loved one is at that moment. The anguish of wondering if they repented or had time to pray in their last moments is rehearsed in their minds a thousand times.

It is unfair to those still living to be troubled with these questions. Confessing Christ is so important, and it is the only way that your family circle will be unbroken for eternity. Your confession seals your prayer of repentance. Even if you struggle from time to time, be swift to pray and sincere to repent. The day will come when you are completely delivered from addictions or bondages. Never give up on God, and He will never give up on you!

CHAPTER 12

DEATHBED REPENTANCE

The story was relayed to me of a family who raised all their children in church, and they seldom missed a church service. As each child matured, a few strayed from the path of their upbringing, sometimes living sinful lifestyles that presented a danger to their eternal destiny.

As one man neared death, he called a sibling so that he could confess his many years of sinful living. Throughout much of his marriage, he had been unfaithful to his wife with numerous women and had done so on a near daily basis. He was now filled with regret and remorse for living a selfish life, and he asked his sibling if God would forgive him for all his sins. The sibling prayed with him, and in his final moments he was at peace with God.

While we rejoice when a sinner repents, an end-of-life confession also brings regret as the person finally realizes they wasted decades living in unrepentant sin and selfishness. Imagine the years of attempting to hide from the Holy Spirit, knowing the truth but not walking in it. The person will have no eternal reward, no crown of righteousness, and no crown of rejoicing. At the heavenly judgment, many will feel shame for not winning others to Christ and for squandering their money and time on themselves and their temporal interests, all the while ignoring Christ until hours before they pierce the veil into eternity. John wrote that we should "abide in Him, that when He appears, we may have confidence and not be ashamed before Him at His coming" (1 John 2:28).

This man's confession and prayer of repentance is considered a deathbed confession. Throughout church history, only God Himself knows the number of people who confessed their sins and asked Christ into their heart at the closing moments of their lives. Some barely made it through heaven's gate, and only because God extended a final act of grace. At the heavenly judgment, many who did nothing for God during their earthly life will see their works consumed to ashes. Paul wrote, "If anyone's work is burned, he will suffer loss; but he himself will be saved, yet so as through fire" (1 Cor. 3:15).

In 1 Peter 4:18, the Apostle Peter posed this question, "And if the righteous one is scarcely saved, where will the ungodly and the sinner appear?" The word scarcely in Greek is *molis*, meaning with great difficulty; with much work. There are many Christians, especially in Western countries, who live a life of spiritual compromise. They walk with one foot barely in the kingdom of God and the other foot in carnal pleasures. If we as Christians scarcely make it into God's kingdom, then the outright sinner and evil transgressor doesn't stand a chance.

IS THIS REPENTANCE BIBLICAL?

A common comment when suggesting the possibility of deathbed repentance is this. Some suggest that, if you did not choose to repent and serve God throughout your lifetime, God will eventually stop convicting you of sin, noting that a person cannot come to Christ unless the Sprit draws them. There are also verses, such as when God told Noah, "My Spirit will not always strive with man..." (Gen. 6:3). In the New Testament, we are told not to grieve or vex the Holy Spirit (Eph. 4:30).

There is one profound example of repentance in the New Testament that was certainly an end-of-life confession. At Christ's crucifixion, alongside Him were two thieves who were sentenced to death. Scripture records the conversation of one belligerent thief on a cross telling Jesus that, if He really is the Christ, He should come off the cross and get the three of them out of this situation. The other thief rebuked this man, reminding him that the two of them deserved their penalty, but Jesus was innocent of any crime. This thief then made a life changing statement to Jesus before he died: "Lord, remember me when You come into Your kingdom" (Luke 23:43).

Jesus replied, "Assuredly, I say to you, today you will be with Me in Paradise" (Luke 23:42). Notice that this man did not repeat a long sinner's prayer with Jesus. He did not present Christ with a verbal list of his lifetime transgressions. His only request was "Remember me when you come into Your kingdom."

What was there about his man's short request that captured the attention of Christ, who followed up by releasing the man from his sins and providing him the path into the eternal kingdom? Scripture tells us what is required for salvation:

> "If you confess with your mouth the Lord Jesus and believe in your heart that God has raised Him from the dead, you will be saved. For with the heart one believes unto righteousness, and with the mouth confession is made unto salvation."
>
> – ROMANS 10:9-10 (NKJV)

First, this man admitted he was a sinner and deserved death (Luke 23:40-41). He then referred to Jesus as Lord; not rabbi (teacher) or even his Jewish name, Yeshuah, but Lord, which identifies Christ as both God and Messiah (Luke 23:42). He acknowledged that Christ was over a kingdom. He asked Christ to remembered him when He came into His kingdom, indicating that the man knew that Christ was not staying in the grave, but would be alive to rule His kingdom. The man did everything the Bible requires for salvation.

Greek scholars teach the true meaning of the word *repentance*. We often associate repentance with begging for forgiveness or repeating all our sins and saying, "I'm sorry" over and over. While this can be part of true repentance, the Greek word refers to changing your thinking to the point that it changes your personal behavior. Many people have asked the Lord to forgive them, yet their sinful lifestyle continues. They have invited Jesus to be their Savior, but they have not made Him Lord over their heart and life through a change in their thoughts and behavior. They want eternal security without personal responsibility.

The thief on the cross is a perfect biblical example of someone who repented just before his death. His confession was not only about his sins, but about his belief in Christ's identity. He and Christ both knew he was a sinner. And the sinner knew that Christ was Lord. He believed in the future kingdom, which means he acknowledged that Christ was not going to remain dead, but He would rise from the dead to oversee a kingdom.

ETERNAL RISK TAKERS

Some individuals have extensive biblical knowledge, can debate scripture, and are experts in judging right and wrong in others. Yet, they refuse to repent of their own sins, choosing instead to risk their eternal souls to maintain the status quo and selfishly serve their carnal lusts and pleasures. Their attitude is, "I'll repent before I die," or "I'll make it right when I'm old, after I've partied."

My response is, "Tell me the year, month, day, and hour when you will die. Tell me how it will happen and where your final breath will be taken." Of course they have no idea. And if they have no idea, then how can they be assured of a chance to repent in their final moments on earth?

Nobody should ever put off salvation, because everybody needs the experience of entering a covenant of eternal life with Christ. Now is the day of salvation (2 Cor. 6:2). Today is the day to choose, because tomorrow could be too late.

SNATCHED FROM THE FLAMES

The following story is an eyewitness account of a death experience, as relayed to me by a ministry partner who worked as a registered nurse.

"One morning about 6 a.m. I was clocking into work at the hospital in Kentucky. My coworkers and I were walking into the unit on the second floor when we all heard the horrible sounds of groaning and moaning coming from a woman in one of the patient rooms. She was hollering at the top of her lungs, "Help me! My feet are on fire!" She yelled the same thing over and over, that her feet were on fire, as she moaned in desperate pain. I immediately went to check the board to see if she was my patient, but she was not.

"I attempted to make rounds on the rest of my patients, but the entire time this same elderly lady kept screaming and pleading for mercy and for someone to help her stop the pain. She repeated that her feet were burning in flames, and that she was being tormented. I went into her room, even though she was not assigned to me, because I sensed a nudge from the Holy Spirit.

"When I walked into her room, I looked at the cardiac monitor and assessed her vital signs. I observed that she had a tachycardia heart rhythm. Her blood pressure and oxygen levels were stable. Other than a fast heart rate and rhythm, she seemed fairly stable.

"I started talking with the lady and asking her how I could help her. She looked at me and began begging me to put out the flames of fire under her covers. When I pulled the covers back, there was no fire that I could physically see with my eyes, and I expressed that to her. Yet, she continued to look at me with an agonizing facial expression and insisted her feet were burning and were on fire.

"I felt from the Holy Spirit that I should ask her if she had a relationship with God. When I began talking about the Lord, she started to cry and tell me that she used to have a relationship with the Lord, but that she had been in a backslidden condition for quite some time, and it caused problems between her and her daughter. At that moment I lead her in a simple sinner's prayer of repentance. She repeated the prayer and immediately began thanking me and praising God, telling me that the fire was out! She wanted me to call her daughter immediately so she could share the good news that she had given her heart to the Lord and received salvation and was free from the fire.

"I walked out of her room to the nurse's station and picked up the phone to call her daughter, when suddenly the monitor started alarming. I went in and observed the lady's vital signs quickly deteriorating.

"My colleagues and coworkers went into her room and kept resuscitating her while I was on the phone with her daughter. The daughter told me that she had been pleading and praying to God for years about her mother returning to the Lord and for Him to have mercy on her. The daughter was so happy to hear that her mom had rededicated her life to God and prayed the sinner's prayer of repentance. The daughter told me she was on her way up to see her mother.

"As soon as the daughter got there, the mom confessed to the daughter that she had given her heart to the Lord. The mother and daughter released forgiveness toward each other, and within minutes thereafter, the woman passed away. I will never forget that experience as long as I live, and I am so grateful that God allowed me to help her pray, repent, and prepare her to escape hell and enter heaven."

This is a clear example of a person near the edge of eternal destruction who comes to their senses, realizes their eternal destination, and makes a last-minute decision to repent, confess, and forgive. In this dying woman's case, God was merciful to have a godly Christian woman on staff at just the right time to boldly minister to her. We also see the importance of having someone stand in the gap and pray for God to save these sinners before they enter eternity.

God was merciful to this woman and answered her daughter's prayer at the last minute. Yet, there could be millions of sinners and backslidden Christians who might never have that same opportunity for an extension of time to suddenly turn back to God.

A similar story with a different ending was relayed to me by another ministry partner who retired from hospital nursing and was eyewitness to the following incident.

"Some patients can be described as rough, and I was assigned to a patient who was especially rough—mean-spirited and foul-mouthed. When I entered her room, she was screaming and hollering that she was hot. She called me the n-word and said, "Don't you touch me!" When I pulled back the covers, her feet were hot and red, and I knew right away that she was feeling the flames of hell.

"When the Holy Spirit would lead me to pray for patients or decree life over them, I always obeyed. Nursing was a ministry

to me; not just a career. I saw patients and hospital personnel accept Christ when I was employed there, and I was blessed to see patients who were expected to die receive healing and be released to go home. When I realized that this woman was dying and going to hell, I told her that I was going to pray for her. She shouted, 'I don't need your prayer!' God told me at that moment that she was a reprobate and there was no point in trying to get her to pray.

"The skin of her legs also began to turn hot and red, as though the flames were moving up her body from her feet. When she shouted, "Leave me alone!" she sounded like a tormented soul. I took her temperature and it registered 109 degrees. I went to the nurse's station and told a doctor about her high temperature, but the doctors always excused an extremely high temperature by saying that the person was suffering from an out of whack body thermostat.

"The woman passed away. It took a while for her body temperature to cool down to a death state. Spiritually, I knew what had happened. She died and opened her eyes in hell. I've experienced situations in the past where someone died, and I was certain they went to hell. But this was one of the worst cases I ever saw."

These two stories reveal similarities but different outcomes. The burning fire was felt by both, but deathbed repentance changed the eternal course for one. The other woman rejected offers of prayer and died without a redemptive covenant with Christ. These two women experienced vastly different eternal destinations once the soul and spirit left their bodies.

I have known of several vehicular fatalities in which the person or persons had a church upbringing and were raised by strong Christian parents, but at the time of their death they were living a carnal life or dealing with weaknesses of the flesh. One promise that has always been a comfort to me reads, "Whosoever shall call on the name of the Lord shall be delivered" (Joel 2:32), and "Whosoever shall call upon the name of the Lord shall be saved" (Acts 2:21). When Peter was drowning, he cried out three words, "Lord, save me" (Matt. 14:30). When a man is drowning in a lake during a storm, he doesn't have time for an extended prayer. Christ responded after three sincere, direct words and Peter's life was spared.

If Christ responded to, "Lord, save me," this same Jesus will hear and respond to a sinner crying out from their heart and mind, "Lord, forgive me." It is not the length of the prayer, but the faith from the heart.

When my grandfather was near death, the doctor told us to speak to him because hearing is the last sense to go. People who have recovered after being unresponsive testify that they could hear conversations, although they were unable to open their eyes or communicate. Despite physical restraints, the person can hear and think. When I spoke to my grandfather, he was unable to open his eyes, yet tears would roll down his face as I spoke. I believe God allows hearing to remain so that someone can pray a prayer and the person can hear the words and agree in their spirit with the prayer.

I would again recommend not risking your eternal destiny with an expectation of last-minute repentance. Two days in the future are unknown—the day of Christ's return, and the day of your death. Watch and pray for the return of Christ, and repent and remain faithful until the end.

CHAPTER 13

RECOVERING FROM THE TRAUMA OF A DEATH

Trauma is defined as severe mental or emotional distress that is caused by a deeply disturbing experience. At some point in life, you will likely experience at least one traumatic event.

You might experience *acute* trauma that occurs from a single incident. Situations such as an unanticipated divorce, an unexpected or violent death that severely impacts the life of a survivor, or the loss of a home or business in a natural disaster are all events that have potential to cause acute trauma.

Continual cycles of physical or emotional abuse, such as domestic violence, childhood abuse, or severe bullying can cause *chronic* trauma to latch onto the individual.

Multiple forms of continual abuse and disturbing experiences lead to the worst form of trauma, called *complex* trauma. An untold number of people have experienced this kind of trauma throughout their lives, and especially their childhood. It might take decades for them to fully recover. Some never do.

People deal with trauma in different ways. Unless we were present to experience it ourselves, we cannot imagine the impact of witnessing a tragic event such as a terrorist attack or a mass shooting. Many people experience nightmares and are struck by a spirit of fear or guilt for seeing people die and being unable to stop the slaughter. This sets a path of trauma in the brain. Some people are so affected, they commit suicide.

I have my own example of how trauma affects the brain, along with the medical report to prove it. I was stuck in a repetitive cycle of always thinking about something negative and traumatic that had happened to me. The result was that it became almost impossible to function like a normal person. I was told about a clinic that a Christian gentleman started, based on principles of science and the way the brain works. It sounded like something that might help me, so I scheduled an appointment.

The first thing they did was test my brain function by using electrodes that also connected to a computer. This revealed that, indeed, my brain was stuck in a path that indicated mental and emotional trauma. The director said to me, "You have been in fight or flight mode for a long time, based on the assessments we're seeing." In a short time, they were able to "reset my brain" by simply using different sounds. The result was that I began to use both sides of my brain in a more balanced manner. I noticed a difference right away and had the medical documentation to prove it.

Your brain can get stuck in a state of trauma and you will find yourself continually thinking of negative or tormenting events and circumstances. Depending on the level of trauma, the emotions a person experiences can range from exhaustion, sadness, anxiety, confusion, agitation, numbness, and dissociation. A sudden death can lead to crying or sobbing in grief, which can last for weeks or months. Even when the person thinks they have recovered, the trauma can be triggered again, causing past events to return to the forefront of thinking.

TRAUMA TRIGGERS

Medical professionals explain that there are *trauma triggers*. The mind is designed to recall events both positive and negative. An example of something triggering you in a positive manner might be walking past a bakery and smelling the scent of baking bread. It might remind you of a thick slice of your grandmother's bread, fresh out of the oven and slathered with butter. Old toys might remind you of the time you had that toy and the ways it engaged your imagination when you were young. A song will bring back a memory of your youth and where you lived or what you were doing the first time you heard the song.

Negative triggers bring back dark or foreboding memories that can be painful to recall. Triggers might include passing the site where a terrible event happened. A trigger might include seeing the same make, model, and color of vehicle the person was driving when a deadly accident occurred. If you grew up in a home where there was verbal or physical abuse and that home still exists, you might drive by the old home decades later and experience uneasiness in your heart or spirit, as terrible memories that had been locked away in your mind suddenly return.

If any type of trauma is not dealt with, it can and will impact a person negatively. I'm convinced, for example, that many of the people who are involved in same sex relationships were themselves emotionally and sexually abused as children, and this caused chronic or complex trauma that affected their lives.

HEALING FOR TRAUMATIC EVENTS

The Christian community is divided over the need for professional counseling. The fact is that we are three-part beings; we have a body, a soul, and a spirit. We have available to us the Bible and the Holy Spirit to deal with issues of the human spirit. But we need to accept the reality that many people are broken in their body, soul, and spirit because they have been hammered with a seemingly endless bombardment of evil, all at the hands of demonically inspired individuals.

Sometimes medical professionals can help bring correction and wholeness in areas that are lacking. A professional counselor can point out problems and advise the person of ways to realign their thoughts and patterns. The worst thing some people ever had to deal with in life is a crazy uncle who started a fight every time he got drunk. People who have spent their lives in a near-perfect environment will have a hard time understanding the paralyzing emotional trauma experienced by someone who has been severely and regularly abused by another person, including a family member in their own home.

Throughout life, I have experienced trauma brought on by the actions of other people, by negative circumstances, and by the deaths of some people. I have received counseling myself to help me through traumatic circumstances. A professional counselor helped me understand the effect of years of rejection from my early teen years and into the early years of my ministry. Understanding the root of some of my conflicts helped me better understand how to use scripture to overcome. I learned to guard my friendships and to carefully select the people I allow within my inner circle. Being on the autism spectrum, I was never able to read the expressions of other people. Counseling also helped me in that area. Of course, I would always recommend that a Christian see a Christian counselor, as they will also understand the spiritual side of our conflicts.

Most people who remain strong in faith, pray, and renew their minds with the Word of God each day will eventually recover from seasons of trauma. In the meantime, there are some exercises that may help you in the process.

1. Write a Letter

If you have been hurt by a person or if you have lost a loved one, sit down and write a letter to the person. That individual doesn't ever have to see the letter, but you can present it to God and tell Him that you forgive the person who hurt you. If you have carried unforgiveness toward that individual, burn or shred the letter as a symbol of closure. If you have lost a loved one, write them a sweet, loving letter and lay it out before God to let Him know how you appreciated their love and their presence in your life. Place it in an old Bible as a symbol of remembrance. This simple act can assist in healing and closure.

2. Pray for The Person(s) to be Healed

When individuals purposely harm or abuse others, as the abusers grow older, they often live with regret over what they did years ago. I know of a situation where a woman in her 60s was molested as a young teenager by a man in her town. Many years later, in a hospital setting, this man apologized and asked the woman to forgive him. As a believer, she had already forgiven him long ago, but she was able to tell the man on the spot that she forgave him. He had lived with shame and guilt for decades, and he told her that he knew what he did was wrong.

Jesus taught us to "pray for your enemies" and to "pray for those who spitefully use you and persecute you" (Matt. 5:44). This prayer is for your benefit as much as theirs. You must forgive others of their trespasses before you can be forgiven of yours (Matt. 6:14-15). Never depart this life with unforgiveness. Deal with the issue now, as holding other people in your mental prison is a dangerous, eternal snare (Matt. 6:12-15).

3. Forgive or Apologize to God

Saying "forgive God" seems odd since we know that God does not tempt people with evil and God cannot sin (James 1:13). Perhaps it is more accurate to say that we need to *apologize to God* for blaming Him for someone's death.

To explain the need to forgive or apologize to God, perhaps this story will illustrate. A woman who is now in her late 40s is also someone I have known since she was three years of age. Years ago, her twenty-year-old brother was suddenly killed in a motorcycle accident.

Her trauma from his death was unbearable. She became angry at God for allowing him to die so young. She turned from the Lord in a season of heartache, and she spiritually rebelled. However, after hearing the Word of God shared with her and understanding that God knows all things, she understood her brother's love for God and God's love for her brother. She returned to Christ and has been a strong Christian to this day. She had blamed God and was unforgiving toward His sovereignty. Thankfully, she learned how to trust instead of blame, which changed her life.

Questioning and blaming God can lead to anger toward Him for allowing the tragedy. This is why we sometimes must forgive God for not stopping the tragedy or apologize to Him for the blame we placed on Him. Not that God needs to be forgiven, of course. What we are doing is mentally and spiritually releasing our heart and soul from blaming Him for a tragic event. You are saying, "God, I am holding nothing against you because you alone are the sovereign God, and you know all things."

4. Trust God Even in Death

A unique biblical narrative conceals important insight. In 2 Kings 20, King Hezekiah became afflicted with a life-threatening disease. The prophet Isaiah instructed him to set his house in order as he was going to die. Hezekiah wept, crying out for God to extend his life. In His mercy, God added fifteen more years to his life.

Here is the twist. After Hezekiah's healing, he was visited in

Jerusalem by men from Babylon. The king freely opened the doors of the holy temple, showing the men all the gold and silver vessels. He allowed them to see the secret wealth of God's house. Because of this one act, Isaiah told the king that he made a terrible blunder. In the future, the Babylonians would invade Jerusalem, seize all the temple treasures, and cart them off to Babylon. This did occur many years later (see Jeremiah 51-52).

Had King Hezekiah died when God originally planned, the Babylonians might have never known what was concealed behind the sacred temple doors. Because Hezekiah lived longer, the king caused Israel years of distress, loss, and captivity. Would it have been better for the king to die and not have an extended life of fifteen more years? What if God, knowing the future, may be allowing a *present* departure to prevent a *future* tragedy?

Christ alone carries the keys of death and hell (Rev. 1:18). When He unlocks the gate on heaven's side and welcomes a faithful disciple home, we on earth must place our complete trust in His sovereignty and timing. He alone sees each person's future, including the snares that could destroy them if they continue in their earthly journey and take a wrong path. Job said it best when he thought he was dying, "Though He slay me, yet will I trust Him..." (Job 13:15). The God you trust in life can certainly be trusted in death.

5. Claim Specific Promises

The promises of the Bible are not activated in your life just because you own five leather copies that are collecting dust in every room in your house, or because you read a few pages occasionally. Promises are activated by faith and by speaking with your mouth the inspired words that are written.

One promise reads, "He heals the brokenhearted and binds up their wounds" (Psa. 147:3). In Christ's first message, He stated that He was sent to "heal the brokenhearted" (Luke 4:18). It is a great heartbreak when death separates us from someone we love. A small piece of our heart is no longer present on earth. The absence of their love, hugs, fellowship, support, and conversation leaves a permanent void. We must confess the verse that God will heal our broken heart and bind up our emotional wounds.

Jesus had a close friendship with Mary, Martha, and Lazarus. When Lazarus died, Jesus wept (John 11:35). Those two words remind us that Jesus understands loss. He knew that He would raise Lazarus from the dead, and He saw the unbelief coming from the sister of Lazarus. However, I believe that those two words are penned in the New Testament to help us understand that Jesus is "touched with the feeling of our infirmities" (Heb. 4:15).

6. Ask God for a Peaceful Closure

People assume that the conclusion of a memorial service should be a time of reflection, memories, and closure for a bereaved family. But sometimes the events surrounding a death do not always bring closure; instead, this initiates a search for answers. If the person was murdered, for example, closure could take years, considering all the investigations and trials that could follow.

When my cousin passed, I could not attend her funeral and I was struggling with closure. I had many questions about the final moments of her life. I wanted to know all the details and I wanted to find the answers, because that's the way my mind works. I wanted to know what happened to cause the man to hit her car, if she was aware of what happened, and how long she lived before she passed away.

Through friends I obtained the full report, including audio. Her car was equipped with OnStar, which automatically called 911 and even recorded the voices of people on the scene. This included audio of a woman telling Louanna to wake up, and a man who was first on the scene attempting to speak to her. I saw a timeline of the chain of events:

12:37 — Call received at the 911 center regarding an accident with entrapment and that the driver is unresponsive.

12:40 — An eyewitness on the scene is at the broken window at Louanna's vehicle, telling her to wake up.

12:46 — Trooper arrives on the scene and transmits that Louanna is in cardiac arrest and a medical helicopter is placed on stand-by.

12:48 — Medical helicopter cancelled and medical examiner is dispatched to the scene due to Louanna being declared deceased.

1:33 — Medical Examiner arrives on scene of accident and officially declares Louanna deceased.

2:14 — Extraction of Louanna's body from the mangled vehicle is completed.

Some people want to know as much as possible, and others don't want to be reminded because the less they know, the faster they can move past the grief. Whether we want more information or less, the fact remains that we cannot bring the person back.

WHAT A MIGHTY MAN OF GOD TOLD ME

Since I was not sensing closure after two months, I called a noted man of God who has an authentic prophetic gift and clearly and accurately hears from the Lord. He has never met me personally and knew nothing about her accident. I told him my cousin had been killed in an accident and asked him to inquire of the Lord to see if God reveals anything to him about the reason behind this accident.

As he began praying and speaking through an interpreter, his prophetic word of knowledge flowed smoothly and swiftly. Within five minutes I had a clear confirmation for why God allowed this to occur. He said twice, "God loved her very much." God's answer to me, through the prophet, was based on Isaiah 57:1, the same verse the Lord had given me in the past regarding death. God was taking her at this time because her future held some great challenges and difficulties. He even revealed the name of a person who would have been linked in the future to certain negative events. This confirmed information that some of her family had considered as well.

Closure does not mean that you close life's book and forget the people you loved. The closure focuses on those "what, when, where, and why" questions. In this life you might never receive a clear answer. When Oral Roberts' daughter and son-in-law were taken in a plane crash, the Lord told Oral that there were things about this that he would never understand in this life, but he would know when he got to heaven.

During this process, the Holy Spirit will continue to speak in a still, small voice asking, "Do you trust me? Do you trust that God knew the future and knew what is best?" The answer is always yes. The Father knows best.

THE ETERNAL LIFE ADVANTAGE

If you as a believer have experienced the death of a loved one, regardless of age, who was a true follower and lover of Jesus Christ and walked in an active covenant relationship with Him, both you and the departed individual have the *everlasting life advantage*. Death is the cessation of this earthy life, while at the same time, it is the beginning of a new life outside the physical body. The soul and spirit of the believer enter the paradise of God, Christ, the holy angels, and the spirits of the righteous men, women, and children who are awaiting the resurrection of the dead.

Death of the earthly physical body introduces eternal life for the soul and spirit that will one day receive a new body. Every believer who has died, whether two years ago or two thousand years ago, has received eternal life. They are waiting for a new glorified body, which they will receive when Christ returns to raise the dead (1 Cor. 15:51-54). Parents, grandparents, close relatives, and friends who have left this earthly realm as redeemed believers in Christ will become part of your future world, if you are among the redeemed.

Paul spoke of this glorious resurrection by reminding the family of God that, without the hope of the resurrection, we would of all men be most miserable. If Christ be not raised from the dead, our preaching is in vain, our faith is useless, and all who have died in Christ would perish (1 Cor. 15:16-19). However, the Bible is clear that because Christ lives, we shall likewise live and live eternally. Through a redemptive covenant with Christ, the grave has no victory and death has no sting (1 Cor. 15:55).

With so many family members already in heaven awaiting their resurrection, you and I must remind ourselves that death was merely a transition from one realm to another, and that all who are in Christ Jesus are more alive now than they were on earth. Their soul and spirit were confined within a house made of clay. At death, their eternal spirit was released from the old house that was filled with pain, suffering, and anguish. Like a bird released from a cage, the soul and spirit received freedom and life everlasting in the presence of God. Absent from the body, they are now present with the Lord (2 Cor. 5:8).

They are not *here,* but they are *there.* Here, their physical shell appears dead as though sleeping. But there, they are completely alive. This is the hope we have. It matters not *how* we get to heaven, whether by death or the return of Christ. It just matters that we make it to heaven.

CHAPTER 14

DON'T GO TO HELL OVER A MYSTERY

Following is a story I read years ago in an Assembly of God publication. When my father was living, he heard me share this moving story and suggested I tell it every time I had an opportunity.

It centers upon a man named Rev. Charles Greenaway, an Assemblies of God minister. In 1940 he married, and the following year, his wife Mary gave birth to a child they named Daniel. At the time they pastored a small, poor congregation in Elba, Alabama. Life was difficult for many people in those days, and pastors received little ministry income. Their faith was stretched just to provide for basic needs, and it took prayer to supply their daily bread.

Charles greatly desired to go to the mission field and minister to people in nations that had not heard the Gospel. However, there was one hindrance. Daniel had been stricken with a serious disease, and treatment was not available on the mission field. The disease required that they remain in the United States so that Daniel could receive care. One hot summer day, Charles and Mary were taking Daniel to a hospital for treatment when their car broke down on the side of the road. He recalled a minister driving past them in his automobile and waving at them.

The Greenaways had seen miracles, knew that God could perform miracles, and prayed for Daniel to be healed. Their prayers went unanswered.

Daniel suffered greatly, and one morning the little fellow passed away. Charles' response was, "God, I know you could have healed Daniel, but you didn't. I don't understand it, but I want you to know that I'll not go to hell over a mystery."

The tragic death of Daniel opened the door for Charles and Mary to become missionaries. Their overseas work began in 1944 when they were appointed to minister to the Mossi tribe on the Ivory Coast of Africa. In 1949 they made a difficult and dangerous journey to Togo-Dahomey, West Africa to minister to primitive tribes.

The Greenaways touched millions of lives, started churches and Bible colleges, and became among the most well-known, respected, and successful missionaries in the Assemblies of God. In his lifetime, Charles Greenaway and his wife Mary touched the world.

When Rev. Greenaway was an elderly minister, he spoke to a missionary friend of mine and requested prayer for his loyal and faithful wife who had become ill. He added, "In all these years, she never got over the death of our son Daniel." Greenaway said that every time they saw a child in need, Mary thought of Daniel.

Mary was a great woman of God who followed her husband into treacherous territory in Africa. Many times, they needed a miracle from God just to stay alive. Yet deep inside her motherly heart, a piece was missing. She lived her entire life knowing that her heart would be made complete when she arrived in heaven and was reunited with her son. Both Charles and Mary passed away and went to heaven the same year, a short time apart.

WHAT DID HIS STATEMENT MEAN?

What did Greenaway mean when he said, "I'll not go to hell over a mystery"? He knew that God *could* heal his son, but God *didn't* heal his son. That is always a mystery for Christians who believe in divine healing.

Why would Greenaway suggest there is a danger of *going to hell* over a situation that was a mystery to him? I suggest the answer is that he knew that he should *not blame God* for failing to heal his boy on this earth. If he chose to blame God, he could eventually become offended with God, which would become a spiritual snare that would lead him into a life of anger and resentment toward God.

A biblical example of offense toward God is when John the Baptist was arrested, at which time he questioned his future and wondered if Christ would be willing to free him from a death by beheading. While in prison, John heard about the works of Christ, so he sent two disciples to ask Christ, "Are You the Coming One, or do we look for another?" (Matt. 11:3). The implied message here is, if You are the One, then get me out of here.

Christ sent word back to tell John, "The blind see and the lame walk; the lepers are cleansed and the deaf hear; the dead are raised up and the poor have the Gospel preached to them (Matt. 11:5). Then came the word, "And blessed is he who is not offended because of Me" (Matt. 11:6).

Jesus was in essence saying, "John, I am the Messiah, and you told your followers that you must decrease and I must increase (John 3:30). Your season has come to an end, and my season must now begin. I am not going to get you out of prison, so don't be offended when I don't do what you want me to do."

The spiritual life lesson is that there are times when we desire God to do one thing, yet He has predetermined to do something else. Many of Christ's first disciples were followers of John the baptizer. John's ministry was to "prepare the way of the Lord and make His paths straight" (Matt. 3:3). Once John prepared the way, then he was to step out of the way.

Imagine the division that might have been created had Christ and John both been in public ministry at the same time. The two were different in many ways. Jesus wore a robe and John was wrapped in camel's hair and a leather belt. Jesus ate fish, while John munched on locusts and wild honey. Jesus spent time primarily in cities and towns; John spent time in the wilderness and baptizing people in water. Each man had a specific season and assignment.

God knew exactly what He was doing. Nobody wants to die by beheading. John the Baptist, Paul, and Peter were executed by beheading. John, who gave us the book of Revelation, was the only disciple who did not die a violent death, although the Emperor Domitian tried to kill him by boiling him in oil. When that failed, John was exiled to the Isle of Patmos.

Early Christians were fed to the lions for sport, burned alive on crosses, and tortured. Paul said that many chose to die in this manner (they did not accept their deliverance) to "obtain a better resurrection" (Heb. 11:35). This refers to receiving the crown of the martyr, the highest reward among the heavenly crowns.

This brings us to four facts of life. We did not select our biological parents. That was God's decision. We did not choose our personal appearance. That was determined for us, and we simply do the best we can with what we were given. Since death and hell are in the hands of Christ (Rev. 1:18), we do not select the moment we die. Finally, we don't choose the way in which we depart for the eternal life to come. It might be through a terminal illness or a tragic accident. Or we might live to be a good old age and pass in the quiet of the night.

No matter what life brings, no matter our circumstances, and despite the fact that death is in our future, there is one unchanging truth: God can be trusted. When Job was in his lowest moment of suffering and despair he said, "Though He slay me, yet will I trust Him" (Job 13:15).

The Hebrew word *slay* is *qatal,* and it means "to put to death." Job's body was suffering from disease, and his friends were telling him that God was behind his suffering and he could eventually die. He argued against their opinion, yet stood firm in saying that, if God did let him die, he would never lose his trust in the Almighty.

The statement may seem cliché, but still it is true. God knows what He is doing — even when we don't think He does. Trust is saying, "*I don't understand it. But I am not going to get angry and offended at God and go to hell over a mystery.*"

CHAPTER 15

YOUR SPIRIT LIVES FOREVER—IN ONE OF TWO PLACES

Two elderly men were discussing life and how fast they went from the vitality of youth to living off vitamins. They discussed morality and how modern technology is researching the use of artificial intelligence to help people live forever. One fellow stared hard at the other and said, "I wouldn't mind living forever; just not in this old body."

We could say the same about living on earth in its present condition. We might not mind living on the earth for a thousand years if earth is not in the same moral and spiritual condition that it is now. If wars, criminal and gang activity, addictions, poverty, and immoral activity ceased, it might be a great place to live for a thousand years. But the world will not change for the better until the return of the Messiah who will clean house by "ruling with a rod of iron" (Rev. 12:5). The day will come when Satan will be bound, and his demonic hordes will be in the abyss for an entire millennium.

Believers in Christ will reign with Him for a thousand years (Rev. 20:6). Some will rule over ten cities, and others will be magistrates over five (Luke 19:11-19). The phrase, "reign with Christ" is a kingly term. Christ will reign as King of kings (Rev. 19:16), meaning that there is no king on earth above Him. Twice in Revelation, the body of believers is referred to as "kings and priests unto God," (Rev. 1:6; 5:10). Overcomers will be rewarded with crowns in heaven for their works on earth, which will also be proof that they are worthy to serve as kings and priests in Messiah's kingdom.

MORTAL VERSUS IMMORTAL

The Apostle Paul revealed that, at the return of Christ, those alive will be changed from mortality to immortality (1 Cor. 15:53). The biblical definition of a mortal is "one who dies." Paul identified the mortal body with a corruptible body (1 Cor. 15:54), a word meaning something that decays or perishes. Something that is *immortal* does not decay.

The idea of a flesh and bones human body being transformed into a resurrected body is called a mystery by Paul:

> *"Behold I show you a mystery, we shall not all sleep but we shall be changed, in a moment, in the twinkling of an eye, at the last trump: for the trumpet shall sound, and the dead shall be raised incorruptible, and we shall be changed. For this corruptible must put on incorruption, and this mortal must put on immortality."*
>
> – 1 CORINTHIANS 15:51-53

The Greek word for *changed* is reminiscent of Christ being transfigured before the eyes of three of His disciples. He was glowing with light, His clothing was white as snow, and His physical countenance shone as bright as the sun. Think of the Greek word *transfigured* as describing a cocoon transforming into a butterfly.

There are two possible life after death finalities—*eternal life* or *eternal punishment* (Matt. 25:46). The Greek word used for eternal in that verse is *aionios*, which means *perpetual, without end, or never ceasing.*

Eternal life refers to the life without end that Christ purchased through His death and resurrection for those who accept salvation. For true followers of Christ, eternal life is a *promise* while living in your physical body on earth, but a *reality* the moment you exhale your last breath. The soul and spirit dwelling within each human are eternal, so once we leave our mortal body, we will find ourselves fully alive and awake in paradise in the third heaven. *Your earthly ending is your eternal beginning.*

The same is true for those who reject salvation through Christ, but their destination is one of eternal punishment. Those who die unsaved, without a redemptive covenant in Christ, will one day breathe their last breath. But they will leave their body and find themselves in a place of darkness and separation from God. The very thought of people, especially those we love, experiencing this judgment is sad and heartbreaking. But the Bible is replete with references to this place called hell.

The word heaven is found in the English translation of the Bible 581 times. The word hell is found fifty-four times. Consistently in scripture, heaven is always located *up,* and hell is always *down* or *beneath.* For example:

- Isaiah 14:9 - "Hell from beneath is moved...."

- Isaiah 14:15 - "You (speaking of Lucifer) shall be brought down to hell."

- Proverbs 27:20 - "Hell and destruction are never full..."

- Isaiah 5:14 - "Hell has enlarged herself, and opened her mouth without measure."

Hell is so difficult to talk about that it seldom comes up in conversation. We might hear the subject of hell discussed after the death of a person who had a reputation for being wicked, belligerent, rebellious, or anti-God. Many people who knew the life of the person understood that, without a last-minute divine intervention and repentance, it is unlikely the person entered heaven.

I have been asked why God would allow the soul and spirit to continue to exist in everlasting punishment. After the great white throne judgment at the end of Christ's millennial reign, death and hell, along with anyone whose name is not found written in the book of life, will be cast into the lake of fire (Rev. 20:14-15). The great white throne judgment reveals the things people did in their lives that kept them from entering the gates of the heavenly city. The antichrist and his companion, the false prophet, will be cast into this fiery abyss where they will be tormented day and night, forever and forever (Rev. 20:10).

This is one of the most troubling parts of the future for those who reject Christ. If we sit and ponder this long enough, most people might question why these sinners can't simply cease to exist, and why their spirits can't evaporate as though they never existed. Some people do believe in eventual annihilation. However, the Bible consistently uses words such as *everlasting* and *forever and forever* when speaking of eternal punishment in hell and the lake of fire.

After studying scripture, I believe this is the answer. Each person is a three-part being; one part is earthly and two are eternal. After death, our earthly physical bodies will, with time, return to the dust (Gen. 3:19). The two eternal parts of our being, the soul and spirit, are created to never cease to exist.

When Adam was created, God formed him using the dust of the earth. Adam came alive only after God breathed into his nostrils the breath of life, and Adam became a living soul (Gen. 2:7). Before Adam and Eve sinned, they could have lived on the earth forever by eating from the tree of life. After they sinned, God said they would die. First they died spiritually, separated from God and the beautiful Garden of

Eden; then they died physically.

Adam's human life lasted 936 years, then he physically died (Gen. 5:5). Yet, Adam has continued to exist in another world for around 5,000 years because his soul and spirit left his body at death. The spirit cannot die because it came from God; He knew us before we were formed and before we came forth from our mother's womb (Jer. 1:5). The spirit that gives us life is the living breath of God. That spirit originated with God, it was formed from God, and it cannot die. God is absolute life, and what comes from Him is also absolute life.

God is a spirit (John 4:24) and angels are spirits (Psa. 104:4). God cannot die and neither can angels—both the faithful angels and the fallen ones—because their spirits are eternal. God placed an eternal spirit inside every human being. Both enter the womb at the moment of conception and bring life to the seed and egg in the mother's womb. A new human life begins; at birth, the umbilical cord is cut to separate the infant from the mother. The new life continues until the body dies physically, at which point the soul and spirit separate from the body and live eternally.

When a believer in Christ dies, we are absent from our body but present with the Lord in paradise in the third heaven (2 Cor. 5:8; 2 Cor. 12:2). Our names are in the Lamb's book of life, which is the heavenly registry that gives the person access to heaven and eternal life.

If the person who died was evil, wicked, refused to repent and change, or walked in biblically forbidden sins, never having those sins washed away by the blood of Christ through repentance, then at death the soul and spirit of this person will go to the underworld. Here there are chambers that confine them under the earth in both darkness and fire. This place of confinement, called hell in English, is also known in Greek by the names Hades, Gehenna, and Tartarus in the New Testament (Matt. 11:23; Matt. 5:29; 2 Pet. 2:4).

Hell was originally prepared for the devil and his angels (Matt.

25:41). The devil led a rebellion against God with a third of the angels, and all were expelled from heaven. Certain fallen angels are presently bound in chains of darkness in Tartarus, which the Greeks considered the lowest hell where the worst spirit beings were confined (2 Pet. 2:4).

Just as a young infant is separated from the mother at birth by cutting a cord, Solomon noted that we experience a strange separation at death. He said that "the silver cord is loosed" (Eccl. 12:6) at the time of death. I have met people who briefly died and then returned to life, and some saw this silver cord when they left their body. When the angel of the Lord severs this silver cord, the spirit of the person is released to leave their body. Immediately their spirit is transported to the other world. In Luke 16:22, when a poor beggar died, the angels carried him to Abraham's bosom.

Eternal means endless and forever. Since your soul and spirit cannot cease to exist, you must choose while you are still alive where your soul and spirit will spend eternity.

THE RICH MAN

A rich man who lived in splendor refused to feed or help a poor man who was covered with sores and begging for crumbs from the rich man's table. When the beggar died, he was carried away to Abraham's bosom. The rich man died and found himself in a state of torment in hell. He could lift up his eyes and see Abraham and Lazarus far away, so he pleaded with Abraham to send the poor beggar back to earth and warn his five brothers not to come to this place.

Abraham noted that the brothers had Moses and the prophets (that is, the Torah and the scrolls of the prophets). If the five brothers did not listen to and heed *their* messages, then the brothers would not be persuaded by someone who comes back from the dead.

Joshua commanded all of Israel, "Choose you this day whom you will serve" (Josh. 24:15). Notice he said *this day*. Eternal decisions must be made *today*, not tomorrow. This is why Paul wrote, "Behold, now is the accepted time; now is the day of salvation" (2 Cor. 6:2). Now is significant, because we have no guarantee that we will wake up tomorrow morning. Christ illustrated this in a parable:

> *"Then He spoke a parable to them, saying: 'The ground of a certain rich man yielded plentifully.*
>
> *"And he thought within himself, saying, 'What shall I do, since I have no room to store my crops?'*
>
> *"So he said, 'I will do this: I will pull down my barns and build greater, and there I will store all my crops and my goods.*
>
> *"'And I will say to my soul, 'Soul, you have many goods laid up for many years; take your ease; eat, drink, and be merry.'*
>
> *"But God said to him, 'Fool! This night your soul will be required of you; then whose will those things be which you have provided?'"*
>
> — Luke 12:16-20

Choose this day. It could be your last day on earth. Just ask the rich man.

CHAPTER 16

PROTECTIVE AND BROKEN HEDGES

Christians often believe that those in covenant with God are automatically surrounded by an invisible hedge that serves as a protective barrier from Satan's assaults. Others believe that each follower of Christ has their own guardian angel assigned to protect and guide them during their lifetime. When a dedicated follower of Christ dies in what seemingly is a premature death, these Christians ask, "What happened to their hedge of protection? Why didn't their angel protect them?"

HEDGES AND ANGELS

The idea of a protective hedge is revealed in the book of Job. Satan attempted to attack Job but was restrained by a hedge that God had placed on Job, his family, and his possessions (Job 1:10).

Here are three facts related to Job's hedge. First, the hedge provided God's protection in every area of Job's life. It covered him, his children, their homes, his livestock, and his health. Second, only with God's permission was Satan allowed to get past this protective barrier to steal, kill, and destroy. Third, even though his children were killed, God placed a restraining order on Satan and refused to allow him to take Job's life (Job 2:6).

Scholars have debated about this hedge. What was it? Apparently it was invisible, and Job did not know it existed; yet both Satan and God knew of its existence. Human eyes cannot see into the spirit realm without God allowing the spiritual veil covering our eyes to be removed (Luke 24:16, 31).

It has been suggested that this hedge was angels that had been assigned to Job, as it is written, "The angel of the Lord encamps round about them that fear Him, and delivers them" (Psa. 34:7). A second example is when Elisha and his servant were protected and surrounded by supernatural horses and chariots of fire (2 Kings 6:17). Angels can serve as protectors of the righteous and prevent danger from being executed against them.

FIVE KINDS OF PROTECTION

From a scriptural perspective, there are five different types of protection.

1. Prayer Coverings

In the Lord's prayer, Christ said to pray that we not be led into temptation and that we be delivered from evil. I have shared how my father prayed daily for our family to be protected from harm, danger, and disabling accidents. In the Old Testament blessing of the high priest, he would speak over the people, "The Lord bless and keep you" (Num. 6:24-26). The Hebrew word keep is *shamar*, and it refers to guarding and hedging about. Christ prayed that God would keep His disciples from evil (John 17:15). This Greek word for keep is *tereo* and it means to guard from loss or injury; to keep an eye upon.

A prayer covering refers to praying and asking God to keep—protect, guard, hedge, and keep an eye upon—you and your family.

2. Angelic Assignments

God can and does assign angels for specific tasks, including commissioning them to observe and protect the righteous. During the Exodus, God revealed to Moses that He was assigning an angel to remain with Israel during their journey to the Promised Land (Exod. 23:23; 32:34). The angel dwelt in the fire and the cloud.

This angel would continue with the people in the wilderness, eventually assisting them in defeating the tribes that were rooted in the Promised Land (Exod. 33:2). The angel was appointed because the people cried unto the Lord and He heard their voice, and sent an angel to bring them forth out of Egypt (Num. 20:16).

We also should ask God for angelic assistance, including when we are traveling. When I fly, I always ask God for His angelic protection while in the air.

3. Inner Warnings

As discussed already, there are times when God will impress a person that there is danger ahead. This manifests as a heaviness that overcomes a person, until it is almost impossible to function as normal because the burden is weighing them down. My father would always pray when his heart became burdened, and in most cases the pressure in his spirit indicated danger in the life of someone he loved. These types of warnings must never be ignored.

4. A Rearward (Rear Guard)

Isaiah 52:12 states that the Lord "will be your rearward." This word, used six times in the Old Testament, means that God is watching your back.

During World War I, military fighter pilots would tell fellow pilots, "I've got your six," meaning "I have your back, so nobody can come upon you from behind." The phrase is still used today. Spiritually, the adversary loves to hit you from behind and blindside you. You'll be having a normal day, when suddenly you are hit with an unexpected attack.

We should always pray for God to protect us in the areas we are unable to see and the situations we are unable to control, so that the enemy cannot blindside us or come up from behind unexpectedly.

5. Wise Decisions

Referring back to a foundational scripture upon which this book is based, Ecclesiastes 7:17 says, "Do not be overly wicked and do not be a fool; why should you die before your time?" Being foolish here refers to making unwise decisions that could and often do lead to danger and death. Illegal drugs, driving while intoxicated, and being caught up in dangerous relationships have ended many lives. We should pray each day and ask the Lord to help us and our family members make wise decisions and avoid possible danger.

All five of these protective strategies can form a hedge around you and your family. We would be astonished if we could observe the discussions in the courts of heaven about God's purposes for us and how the adversary plots against us. We might also be surprised to learn the many times we have been protected, although we were unaware of the invisible angelic messengers assigned to preserve us.

BROKEN HEDGES

What might we do that causes a dangerous crack in a protective hedge? Solomon wrote, "He who digs a pit shall fall into it; and whoever breaks a hedge, a serpent shall bite him" (Eccl. 10:8). In ancient times, stones were used to build walls of protection, and most homes were built with rocks from the local area. Serpents hid in stones and rock walls. If a person were to carelessly begin to remove the stones, they could easily be bitten by a hidden serpent.

Breaking a hedge can certainly occur when a person willfully ignores biblical warnings to repent and change their behavior. Clinging to unrepentant sin or continuing in a sin cycle will eventually catch up with a person, as God warns, "Be sure your sin will find you out" (Num. 32:23). Abel's brother, Cain, was warned when he became jealous over Abel's offering that, if he did not do right, sin was lying at his door (Gen. 4:7).

All the enemy needs to enter your life is a crack large enough for a snake to slither through. Once you have been bitten by the influence of the adversary, your hedge of protection is weakened. And if you are digging a pit, hoping that someone you don't like will fall into it, you will end up falling into it yourself. Look what happened to Haman when he built the gallows for the Jews, and then he and his sons were hung on their own gallows (Esther 9:13).

Willful disobedience against God eventually weakens any hedge and can hinder spiritual or physical protection.

YOUR CHILDREN AND THE HEDGE

Many Christian parents have engaged in intense intercession for God to show mercy upon a straying child. Years ago, when my son lived at home, he experienced a long season of drug and alcohol addiction. Our young daughter was also at home, and my wife and I were concerned, not only for the spiritual and physical condition of our beloved son, but about how his decisions might impact his sister. I remember discussing what could occur to our son if he were on his own and learning through tough love how to live outside the security of our home.

I rejected the idea of kicking him out of the house. With this kind of bondage, I knew that the enemy would play on his mind, and he could end up overdosing or becoming depressed and ending his life. The revelation I received was that our home was dedicated to God, and we were under a hedge of God's grace and protection. As long as our son was living upstairs in our home, he also was under the family hedge of protection.

God's favor, grace, and blessings are part of His covenant with us. Protection is part of God's relationship with those who dwell in the secret place of the Most High (see Psalm 91). For our lives to be extended and protected, a divine hedge is necessary. We can obey the scripture and maintain this hedge, while at other times our disobedience could weaken the hedge.

There will even be times, such as in Job's example, when God may allow the adversary a season to test us or even to realign us, and the hedge will be lifted. However, in the end, God turned Job's captivity and blessed him with double, returning the hedge of protection and all that he owned. In the end, Job and God won.

For a believer, even when deadly tragedies occur, we win because our destination is heaven. Once there, the deceased would never want to return to earthly challenges. They will not return to us, but we can go to them (2 Sam. 12:23).

CHAPTER 17

BE QUIET! DON'T SAY IT!

Words are powerful. They even hold the power of life and death (Prov. 18:21). Jesus taught that, if two on earth agree concerning anything they ask, it will be done for them by my Father in heaven (Matt. 18:19).

This principle works in both the positive and negative realms. To receive salvation, the Holy Spirit baptism, healing, or any spiritual gift, the path to receiving begins by asking in prayer.

Believers talk about our "confession." A confession is simply the words you speak—the words you confess—that maintain your confidence in the prayer you have prayed. Your confession should be spoken aloud and spoken in faith. Once we pray, we must "hold fast (seize; hold onto) the confession of our faith without wavering" (Heb. 10:23).

We have all encountered Christians who constantly confess their fears and all the negative things they believe will happen to them or other people. After Job mourned the death of his ten children and the loss of all his wealth, he said in Job 3:25, "For the thing which I greatly feared is come upon me, and that which I was afraid of is come unto me." Job had been concerned about his children cursing God. He continually made a sacrificial offering to cover for the possibility of this sin (Job. 1:5). Satan observed Job's actions, including his fears, and based a severe attack on his hope that Job would curse God (Job 1:11; 2:5).

Fear can be discerned by both angelic and demonic spirits that operate throughout the spirit world. Satan heard Job confess his fear (Job 3:25), then knew where and how to attack this righteous man.

HUNG BY YOUR TONGUE

We need to reject our fear and speak out our faith. Three biblical books—Psalms, Proverbs, and James—all tell the readers of the blessings or curses and the positive or negative outcomes that are carried in the power of our words. All tell us the power and the dangers of a negative tongue.

James wrote that if believers do not control their tongue, then their religion is in vain (James 1:26). Solomon said that "death and life are in the power of the tongue, and they that love it will eat the fruit thereof" (Prov. 18:21). The truth of how *life* is in the power of the tongue is evident by the fact that eternal life comes through repentance of your sins and confession with your mouth. This is how we are saved, as it is written, "With the heart man believes unto righteousness and with the mouth confession is made unto salvation" (Rom. 10:10).

Death is also in the power of the tongue. Consider how nations engage in war by planning their assaults in war rooms, discussing their strategies with words. Dictators command armies of destruction with words. Angry words have set emotions on fire, sending a person to an early grave with a gunshot wound or even road rage.

THE DANGER OF IDLE WORDS

On a practical level, Christ spoke firmly about the words we speak. He said, "By your words you will be justified, and by your words you will be condemned" (Matt. 12:37). Christ revealed that when we stand before Him at the judgment seat, "Every idle word that men shall speak, they shall give account thereof in the day of judgment" (Matt. 12:36). The word *idle* refers to words that are unfruitful, ineffective, and worthless. This same word is used in Christ's parables when unemployed people were standing idle in the marketplace (Matt. 20:3, 6).

Most of my family was originally from or presently lives in West Virginia. Small town mountain folks are a closely knit group with great hospitality. In most convenience stores, older ladies at the cash register greet all the customers by calling them honey, sweetie, or darling. Many of these precious folks, especially the older citizens, were raised in families where men worked in the coal mines. Many were raised in households of poverty. In early days, many had no indoor restrooms or plumbing. My cousin Louanna and her siblings took a bath in the river when the reservoir dried up in the summer. With ten children in the family, at times their mother mixed a can of evaporated milk with water to make milk for everybody.

Louanna loved Jesus, seldom missed a church service, and supported ministries financially. She identified herself as "just a hillbilly." You never had to guess what she was thinking. She had quick wit and was outspoken at times. Mountain folks often have their own language and opinions that might be offensive to some.

I once shared with her the verse on idle words, advising her that a person doesn't always have to comment or give their opinion. At times it's best to say nothing. Sometimes I would say to her, "Don't say it. Don't say anything." You won't have to apologize for what you never said, and you won't have to answer for idle words you never spoke.

Your words can help you, distract you, or defeat you. Some families or cultures are prone to having quick wit or a quick temper. But we cannot make excuses that it's "in our genes." We should take responsibility for our words and actions and "be angry and sin not," and "do not let the sun go down upon your wrath" (Eph. 4:26).

People tend to soften as they grow older because age brings maturity, maturity brings wisdom, and wisdom teaches that there is no value in engaging in some battles. Refuse to fight something you are not assigned to fight, and don't be pulled into another person's offense. Once people allow themselves to be pulled in, they will find themselves engaging in gossip, criticism, and verbal attacks, thereby paying no attention to the idle words that will come back on them at the judgment. It might also come back on them here on earth, as they later regret things they've said. Once they've said it, they can't take it back.

BEWARE OF SPEAKING DEATH

Christians should always confess and speak life and never death. Sometimes when family members passed away with a certain disease, we hear those who are living confess, "It will probably happen to me, too." Perhaps you have said, "Mom (or Dad) died in their sixties, and I'll probably be gone by then, too." We confess our fears, such as the fact that we're afraid to fly because the plane might crash, or we're afraid to drive because we might be involved in an accident.

God operates through faith, and the adversary moves into your life through fear. There is a godly fear that is defined as a deep reverence for God. However, there is a *spirit of fear* that does not come from God (2 Tim. 1:7). Faith attracts God, while fear alerts the kingdom of darkness of the potential ways to attack us.

For several years, I prayed for a serious family situation. Without realizing it, I wavered for almost nine years. The book of James noted that a person who wavers (doubts) cannot receive anything from God (James 1:6). Here is how I wavered. One day I would pray in faith, then days later I would speak in unbelief. My prayer would be, "Lord, I am believing you will do this..." Days later I confessed, "I don't know why nothing is happening. Where is the breakthrough? Will this ever happen?"

One day the Spirit of the Lord convicted me by saying, "Stop aborting your breakthrough." Immediately I began to replay in my mind the years of *prayers* versus my *confession*. My faith dominated my prayers, but my doubt dominated my confession. My prayers revealed what I desired, but my confession revealed my wavering.

The heart believes (holds a key), and the mouth confesses (opens the door). A closed heaven and lack of answers may not be because of your lack of prayer; it could be that your negative confession is a roadblock to your answer.

The purpose for teaching this is to emphasize the importance of *guarding the words* that proceed from your mouth, as they could undermine your length of days. Life and death are in the *power* of the tongue (Prov. 18:21). The word *power* used here is the Hebrew word *yad*, and the symbol of the letter yad in Hebrew is a *hand*. We could say, the power of things pertaining to life and death are in the hand (or control) of the tongue.

My Jewish guide in Israel noted that when infants come into the world, they enter with a clenched fist. The Jewish sages say this is because they know they can have everything. When we die an old man, we die with an open hand because we can take nothing with us. The righteous followers of Christ can take something with us, though. We can take souls. I once said, "There is something better than heaven and something worse than hell." What could be better than heaven? It is to win lost souls and meet them in heaven. Something worse than hell is to go there and know that you have influenced others, through your rebellious attitude, your unforgiveness, and your careless living, to follow in your footsteps, all the way to your final destination.

CHAPTER 18

MANY ARE SICK AND WEAK, AND MANY SLEEP

Paul wrote in 1 Corinthians 11:29-30, "For he that eateth and drinketh unworthily, eateth and drinketh damnation to himself, not discerning the Lord's body. For this cause many are weak and sickly among you, and many sleep. For if we would judge ourselves, we should not be judged."

First Corinthians chapter 11 contains remarkable spiritual revelations that Paul wrote to the church at Corinth, Greece. In this chapter he set guidelines for the Eucharist (Communion) that celebrates the blood of Christ for our salvation and the body of Christ for our healing. He warned that Christians who partake of this sacred meal in an unworthy spiritual condition could unleash damnation upon themselves. The word damnation is the Greek word *krima*, which means "punishment or a judicial judgment for or against something."

By not properly judging yourself and repenting for sins you may be dealing with, including sins such as bitterness, envy, or unforgiveness, you have taken the Communion meal unworthily, or as the Greek word *anaxios* expresses, "irreverently." Irreverently means "treating as a common meal, not apprehending the solemn symbolic importance of the bread and cup." The result is that, instead of the Lord's Supper bringing life and healing, the person can experience weakness, infirmity, or in rare instances, sleep, which is a metaphor for death. As believers partake of this meal, we are to judge ourselves to ensure that we have repented of any sin. "For if we would judge ourselves, we should not be judged" (1 Cor. 11:31).

A similar situation occurred with the ark of the covenant, which was the gold covered box that contained three sacred items and was carried by four priests. These priests were set apart and divinely appointed to transport God's presence. However, if anyone other than these priests carelessly touched the Ark, that person would instantly die (2 Sam. 6:6-7). The same presence of God on the Ark that defeated Israel's enemies in battle could have the opposite effect and bring sudden judgment on anyone who abused the divine order.

In 1 Corinthians 11:30, the Greek word for weak is *asthenes* and refers to "being feeble or without physical strength." The word sickly is *arrostos* in Greek and it speaks to an absence of health or having some type of infirmity.

Paul spoke of those who sleep. In the context used here, sleep does not refer to lying on a bed taking a nap or resting for the night. Paul spoke of the death of a Christian using the metaphor "sleep." When Lazarus died, Jesus said, "Lazarus sleepeth" (John 11:11 KJV). John explained, "Howbeit, Jesus spoke of his death: but they thought he had spoken of taking a rest in sleep" (John 11:13). Paul spoke of David sleeping in Acts 13:36, "For David, after he had served his own generation by the will of God, fell on sleep, and was laid unto his fathers, and saw corruption."

Early Christians noted that when a fellow believer died, they assumed a physical appearance as if they had fallen asleep. First Corinthians 11:29-30 indicates that some within the church had died before their appointed time by not discerning the body of Christ.

The church at Corinth was judging others but not judging their own sins. In this case, the issue deals with the sacredness of the

Communion meal. The meal was served to remind Christians of Christ's death and suffering and to ensure that each person turn the inspection mirror inward, letting go of any sin or spiritual weight that was hindering their walk with Christ. Discerning the body, first and foremost, means to discern the importance of Christ's suffering and death on the cross—healing for the body and salvation of the soul. The church is called the Body of Christ. We are to love the church as we love ourselves or our companion. Whatever we do to the Body of Christ is the same as doing it to Christ's body.

THE SLEEPING SAINTS

Partaking of the Lord's Supper should inspire us to examine our own life and see if there is sin in our life for which we need to repent. Unless we repent, we risk being "chastened of the Lord, that we should not be condemned with the world" (1 Cor. 11:32). This type of self-judgment and repentance helps keep sin, iniquities, and transgressions out of our lives, as we understand that willful disobedience is the crack in the door that releases negative consequences against our flesh (weakness, sickness, and possibly death).

FELLOWSHIPPING IN OFFENSE

From my own observation, may I suggest that the greatest sin in the church today is that of unforgiveness. Pride is the root of many sins, as often it is pride that keeps us from doing what is right. I once heard a minister's wife say, "If my husband is wrong about something he says or does, he will never admit he was wrong. He has too much pride."

For decades, I have warned Christians of the seriousness of linking arms with others in their offense against other Christians. Just as it is possible to be "joined with a harlot as one body, becoming one flesh"

(1 Cor. 6:15-16), this idea of "one flesh" will cause you to form a soul tie with another person in their offense. But it won't end there. You are now one flesh in agreement with a spirit of confusion. Coming in agreement with someone's offense joins you together with that person so that you also experience their problems and hindrances, as well as take on their spirits.

Many pastors have watched one or more married couples leave a church in anger over an offense, then pull others into their offense. Within two years, couples who joined their offense begin to experience marital problems. Families become divided. Children leave the faith and choose sinful or alternative lifestyles. Ringleaders of offense become afflicted with a disease. Over time, others who joined in the offense become afflicted with disease and infirmity. It is dangerous for your family, your health, and even your life to fellowship in offense.

Christians sometimes have their own personal list of acceptable and unacceptable sins. Acceptable sins are the ones they believe they have a justifiable reason to commit, regardless of what the Bible says. Repent of *all* sin, including those you feel justified holding onto. Don't open the door to the possibility of becoming sick, weak, or even cutting your life short.

Only God knows all the things people have done to hinder their spiritual breakthroughs. Learn from the mistakes of others, stay humble before God, keep your heart pure, and keep a repentant spirit. Do not let the sun go down upon your wrath (Eph. 4:26). By remaining pure in mind, body and spirit, you help God extend His promise of a long life. The Lord's Supper does have the authority to heal, if it is properly received and if we understand the atoning and healing work of Christ through the shedding of His blood.

CHAPTER 19

THE DANGER OF OFFENDING YOUR ANGEL

I n the realm of the spirit, it is possible to offend the Holy Spirit, as it is written, "grieve not the Holy Spirit" (Eph. 4:30). In the wilderness, Israel offended God with their unbelief, as God revealed in Psalm 95:10 that He was grieved with this generation for forty years. Unbelief was also an issue among Christ's disciples, as noted when Christ rebuked the group because of their unbelief (Mark 16:14).

Many Christians have never heard of the possibility of offending an angel. Yet, we will see from scripture that offending an angel is not only possible but could prevent that same angel from providing protection.

There is not a specific scripture using the phrase "guardian angel." However, God's angels do provide protection. Psalm 34:7 tells us that "the angel of the Lord encamps around them that fear the Lord and delivers them." Children were present when Christ was preaching and said, "In heaven their angels do behold the face of the Father in heaven" (Matt. 18:10) Christ warned of great danger to anyone who would offend a child. When you offend a child, you offend the angel assigned to that child.

In the first chapter of Exodus, Pharaoh demanded that every newborn Hebrew boy be thrown alive into the Nile River to kill them. Later, when the angel executed justice, God avenged the children by sending Pharaoh into the Red Sea, drowning him and his army. In Acts 12, Herod beheaded the Apostle James. Days later, during a parade, an angel of the Lord struck Herod and he was eaten by worms. Some suggest the angel that delivered Peter was the angel that executed judgment because of Herod beheading James.

OFFENDING THE DELIVERING ANGEL

Two verses speak to the fact that an angel can be offended. The first passage is insight from King Solomon:

> *"Be not rash with thy mouth, and let not thy heart be hasty to utter anything before God: for God is in heaven, and thou upon the earth: therefore, let thy words be few."*
>
> — ECCLESIASTES 5:2 (KJV)

> *"Suffer not thy mouth to cause thy flesh to sin; neither say thou before the angel that it was an error: wherefore should God be angry at thy voice, and destroy the works of thine hands?"*
>
> — ECCLESIASTES 5:6 (KJV)

In 1 Chronicles 21:1, Satan provoked David to number the men of war in Israel. David assigned this task to his military commander Joab, but David made a serious mistake. The Torah instructed that, when a census was conducted, each man had to give a half-shekel ransom offering to the Lord (Exod. 30:12-13). Not doing so would bring a plague among them.

David omitted this important requirement and never collected the redemption price. Consequently, a *destroying angel* was commissioned to plague the men of Israel, leaving a trail of 70,000 dead men in his path. *The sin of one man impacted the lives of many men.*

The entire nation of Israel was kept from entering the Promised Land, and they wandered unnecessarily because of words of unbelief uttered by ten of the men who had been sent to spy out the land (Num. 13). Nine times God noted that Israel had secretly murmured (in their tents) and He heard it. The word murmur means to complain with your mouth, to blame, or to grumble. Their grumbling centered around God's decisions, with which many disagreed. Their negative remarks spread unbelief among the entire encampment, infecting hundreds of thousands at once. Only two of the spies, Joshua and Caleb, maintained their faith. Both men had another spirit, or a different attitude (Num. 14:24).

God had warned the Israelites about sin in their camp and the impact it would have. An angel was assigned by the Lord to direct the Israelites through the wilderness to the Promised Land. They saw a pillar of cloud during the day and fire glowing in the night. Exodus tells us:

> "Behold, I send an Angel before thee, to keep thee in the way, and to bring thee into the place which I have prepared. Beware of him, and obey his voice, provoke him not; for he will not pardon your transgressions: for my name is in him. But if thou shalt indeed obey his voice, and do all that I speak; then I will be an enemy unto thine enemies, and an adversary unto thine adversaries. For my angel shall go before thee ..."
>
> – EXODUS 23:20-23 (KJV)

According to the revelation given to Moses, this mysterious angel dwelt in the pillar of cloud positioned above the tabernacle, enabling him to continually view the Israelites through the cloud (Num. 20:16, Num. 9:15-18, Ex. 14:19). He was called the "angel of the presence" (Exod. 33:14). God called him, "Mine angel," or we could say he was God's personal messenger. Moses said that the name of God was in him.

If the people offended this angel through their disobedience, disdain, and rebellion, then this angel was given the authority to retain their sins and unleash judgment. God referred to the stubborn people as rebels and stiff-necked (Num. 17:10, Ex. 32:9, Ex. 33:3-5).

At the edge of the Promised Land, ten men ruined the faith and hope of hundreds of thousands by speaking doubt and unbelief toward God's ability to perform His word. This sin of unbelief offended the angel of the Lord, causing him to send the Israelites wandering in the desert.

At the conclusion of forty years, Joshua met this angel when He arose near Gilgal and saw a man with a drawn sword. The angel called himself the captain of the army of the Lord (Josh. 5:15), and he revealed to Joshua the strategy for conquering Jericho (Josh. 6).

This angel could not perform his assignment of bringing the people into their promised possession, because the sin of unbelief was so severe that it took four decades to clear the guilt of the fathers and mothers and allow the children to inherit the land. It took an entire generation for God to remove the reproach from a generation that failed because of unbelief and murmuring.

The people offended the angel of His presence. They provoked—meaning they vexed and grieved—the Lord. Their mouths caused them to sin. They had sinned against the Word of God, weakening God's promises in the eyes of the people by:

- complaining about eating the manna God sent to them (Num.11:4-9)

- Miriam publicly ridiculing the Ethiopian wife of Moses (Num. 12:1-3)

- the ten spies complaining that the giants were too big to conquer (Num. 14:1-12)

- complaining that Moses was taking on too much power (Num. 16:1-27).

When the nation offended the angel, the hedge of God's favor was removed. The men went to battle and lost. The same thing happened after they conquered Jericho. Israel was in covenant with God. Any covenant that God makes between Himself and an individual or group has legal ramifications. Obey the covenant and be blessed. Break the covenant and suffer the consequences.

We must continually guard our mouth. Our spoken words activate movement within the kingdom of God or the kingdom of darkness. When your heart believes the Word and your mouth confesses the Word, you create faith.

Jesus said that your mouth will either justify or condemn you at the heavenly judgments (Matt. 12:37). Eternal life is received through confession—that is, the power of your tongue (Prov. 18:21). We overcome Satan by the blood of the Lamb and the testimony of our mouth (Rev. 12:11). Demonic spirits are expelled from humans through speaking the name of Jesus. Words also have the power to create destruction.

FIVE THINGS THAT CAN OFFEND AN ANGEL

The Bible tells us five things that can offend an angel of the Lord: wrong words, unbelief, sin, not giving God the glory, and disobedience to God's Word.

1. Wrong Words

Eight chastisements were sent against the Israelites in the wilderness, all because of the abuse and misuse of their words:

- God sent a fire when the people complained (Num. 11:1-3).

- God sent a plague when they complained about eating manna (Num. 11:4-35).

- God sent leprosy as punishment for speaking out against Moses (Num. 12:1-16).

- God sent death for grumbling and complaining against God (Num. 14:27-35).

- God sent sickness for their unbelief when they grumbled and complained that they could not enter the Promised Land (Num. 13:31-33).

- God sent an earthquake for complaining against Moses and Aaron (Num.16:29-33).

- God sent a plague because the people grumbled and complained against Moses and Aaron (Num. 16:41-50).

- God sent fiery serpents because the people spoke against Moses and God (Num. 21:5-9).

In each instance, it was complaining, criticism, and murmuring that opened the door to God's anger, resulting in severe chastisements and judgments. Once again, this proves that life and death are in the power of the tongue. *By offending God's angel, an entire generation lost their inheritance.*

2. Unbelief

Unbelief causes a person to come short of God's promises (Heb. 4:1), hinders prayers (Matt. 17:20), and eventually can lead to spiritual separation from God.

Jesus continually rebuked His own disciples for their unbelief (Mark 16:14). This is not a sin of the flesh, but a sin of the spirit. It will hinder your miracle, the answers to your prayers, and all spiritual blessings. Many who have heard the message of Jesus and have not received Him have a root of unbelief.

A unique story in Luke 1:5-20 illustrates how unbelief impacts the angelic world. Zechariah was a priest at the temple in Jerusalem. While offering incense at the golden altar, he saw and heard the angel Gabriel give him a prophecy that he and his elderly, barren wife Elizabeth would have a son named John, who would minister in the spirit and power of Elijah. Zechariah was wavering in unbelief, so he asked the angel for a sign that his words were true. This provoked Gabriel, who told the doubting priest, "Because you believed not my words, you will go speechless for nine months."

Near the same time in Nazareth, the virgin Mary received a visitation from the same angel, Gabriel, telling her that she would have a Son, she would call His name Jesus, and He would save the people from their sins. Instead of questioning the accuracy of the prophecy, Mary said, "Be it unto me according to your word" (Luke 1:38)

God cannot and will not honor unbelief, as unbelief is an enemy that stops miracles and hinders answers to prayer. When we pray, we are to "ask in faith, nothing wavering." Even Christ could do no miracles in Nazareth because of their unbelief (Matt. 13:58). Demons are free to remain inside their victim if an exorcism is performed in unbelief (Matt. 17:20).

We find other scriptures concerning ancient Israel's attitude toward God:

"And they sinned yet more against Him by provoking the Most High in the wilderness" (Psalm 78:17).

"And they tempted God in their hearts by asking meat for their lust" (Psa. 78:18).

"They spoke against God saying, can God furnish a table..." *(Psa. 78:19).*

"Because they believed not in God and trusted not in His salvation" *(Psa. 78:22).*

"Yet, they tempted and provoked the Most High God..." *(Psa. 78:56).*

"For they provoked Him to anger..." *(Psa. 78:58).*

"They tempted God and limited the Holy One of Israel" *(Psa. 78:41).*

Ancient Israel serves as our example. We should not fall into the same sins that they did, and thereby fall short of God's blessings, promises, and life.

3. Sin

In John 5:1-9, there was a natural spring with five porches at the sheep market in Jerusalem. John said that an angel came down at a certain season and troubled the water, and the first person in the water was instantly cured of whatever infirmity afflicted them. When Christ arrived, He never used the water, nor did He ask for a visitation of a healing angel. He healed the man with His words. Later, Jesus told the man to go and sin no more, lest a worse thing come upon him (John 5:4-14).

Here are three biblical truths that should help a Christian reject the offer or temptation to sin. First, the Holy Spirit is in us, and sin will vex or grieve the Spirit of God (Eph. 4:29-32). Second, holy angels are assigned to our life and can be present, watching at the time we are acting up and acting out. Third, Paul said we are surrounded by so great a cloud of witnesses, and we should lay aside every weight and the sin that so easily ensnares us, and run our race with endurance (Heb. 12:1-2).

Even when people do things in secret, there is always someone watching in the spirit world—even the enemy. The Bible tells us that Satan tempted Jesus (Luke 4), he targeted Peter (Luke 22:31-34), he entered the heart of Judas (Luke 22:3), and he motivated Ananias and Saphira to lie to the Holy Ghost (Acts 5:3). Abiding in unrepentant sin is always a spiritual roadblock.

4. Not Giving God the Glory

Two men refused to give God the glory, resulting in an angel executing a serious judgment on both. One was King Nebuchadnezzar who constructed Babylon. The proud and arrogant king was full of himself, and the prophet Daniel ordered the king to humble himself. If he did not, God would send an angel of judgment and inflict a seven-year mental breakdown. Daniel 4:16-17 says that the decision to send the king into mental and political exile was "the decree of the watchers." The watchers were guardian-type angels that had observed the king's actions and made a decree against the king.

One year after the warning, the king stood on his balcony saying, "Is this not the Babylon that I have made with my own hands, for my honor and my glory?" (Dan. 4:30). Immediately, a voice from heaven warned him that he was finished as king. He was driven from the palace and lived like a wild beast for seven years (Dan. 4).

Another was Herod, who was unrepentant after beheading James and had no remorse about plotting the death of Peter. A short time later, a heavenly decree was made against Herod that would remove him from this life. If Herod had continued to remain in authority, he could have arrested and executed other church leaders. Acts 12:23 tells us, "And immediately the angel of the Lord smote him because he gave not God the glory: and was eaten of worms and gave up the ghost."

The Jewish historian Josephus wrote that Herod fell into the deepest sorrow. A severe pain arose in his bowels, and he died after five days of illness. Herod was in a parade, dressed in a silver garment that shimmered from the sun reflecting on the bright metal. People began exclaiming, "He is a god! He is a god!" Then Herod doubled over in pain. He took glory from God. At times, angels executed God's judgment on arrogant leaders.

5. Disobedience to God's Word

This example comes from Numbers 23. It occurred after Israel was released from Egyptian captivity, when a seer named Balaam was offered payment to stand on a hill and curse the Israelites. Balaam was warned twice not to go or attempt this act. But after being pressured by the King of Moab, Balaam consented.

Along the journey, an angel of God blocked the path, preventing Balaam's donkey from passing. The animal saw the angel and was frightened, crushing Balaam's foot against a wall. The reason for this angelic resistance is found in Numbers 22:32, "I went to withstand you because your way is perverse." Balaam's name goes down in scripture as a compromiser.

At times, even righteous people can become angry enough to cause problems. On two occasions, Moses was used to bring water in the desert—in Rephadim (Exod. 17:1-7) and in Kadesh Barnea, thirty-eight years later (Num. 20:1-12). In Rephadim, he stood, held up his rod, and water flowed from a massive rock. The second time he was told to *speak* to the rock, but instead, in anger he hit the rock twice. The first time he simply prayed and obeyed God. The second time he said, "Must we fetch you water from the rock?" (Num. 20:10).

While touring Petra in Jordan, my Arab guide pointed out, "Moses' sin was not hitting the rock twice. God said it was because he did not glorify God in the eyes of the people, but with his words made it appear that Moses was the people's source, and that without him, they would have no water. Moses' wrong actions cost him the opportunity to cross the Jordan and enter the Promised Land.

In a previous chapter, I mentioned my dad's half-brother, Morgan. In November of 1949, Morgan attended a revival and accepted Christ. Morgan invited Dad to the revival, and he went and received Christ. Dad never looked back. However, Morgan experienced an embarrassing offense in a church where he was publicly reprimanded, even though the pastor's intoxicated son was at fault. Morgan left the church after that and never returned. For forty years, he was a backslider with no interest in eternal consequences.

When Dad saw the vision of Morgan being killed in the highway accident, he asked God to send an angel to protect Morgan. The Lord spoke troubling words to Dad and said, "Morgan has chosen to willfully reject me and turn from my covenant, and he is not under my protection." As Dad continued to intercede and plead for Morgan's life, the Lord spoke and said, "I assigned an angel to you years ago. Ask me to send your angel to protect Morgan and I will spare his life." Dad began interceding powerfully for God to immediately send an angel to wherever Morgan was.

While Dad was praying, Morgan and his driver were on the road. Morgan felt a sudden urge to stop at a store, but once inside he couldn't remember why he stopped. He was inside only briefly before he got in the car, and he and the driver headed back down the road.

As they rounded a curve, they came upon an accident. Morgan's neighbors had been driving behind them, but when Morgan stopped the car, the neighbors continued down the winding, two-lane road. A loaded coal truck had crossed the line and hit the neighbor's car head-on. Both the husband and wife were killed instantly.

Morgan had an appointment with death that day, and intercession stopped it. Dad believed the angel sent by the Lord put it in Morgan's mind to stop for a few minutes to prevent his death.

WHERE WAS THEIR PROTECTION?

Thousands of Christians have been taken to heaven after a fatal accident. When this happens, often the first question asked is, "Why didn't God protect them? Why didn't God send an angel to stop this?"

Using my father's and my own personal experiences, I know it is possible to override warnings that come through your spirit. Perhaps the person felt they should not travel that day, or they may have been warned by others. Instead of listening, they ignored the warning and continued with their plans.

On April 19, 1995, something horrific was planned at the Alfred P. Murrah Federal Building in Oklahoma City. Before the workday began, the mother of a woman who worked in the federal building was heavily burdened with a sense of foreboding disaster. She had been praying all morning and told her daughter not to go to work that day. The mother and daughter prayed together about it, but the daughter went on to work and placed her own young daughter in the daycare center located on the first floor of the federal building.

Not long after she had gotten to her office, a call came from the daycare center asking that she please come and get her daughter. She was screaming and crying uncontrollably, causing the other children to be disruptive as well. The child's mother decided to take her home for her mother to care for that day.

As she drove away, bombs exploded at the federal building. The blast killed 168 people, including nineteen children. Hundreds more were injured. The daughter and her child were spared, but both could have been killed. What if the mother had ignored the burden that morning? What if they had not prayed? What if the daughter had ignored the pull to take her child to her mother's home that morning?

We might not know the answers to some questions until we enter eternity, when all things will be understood. We won't know what God or an angel that He sent may have attempted to do to prevent a tragedy, but the person involved may have been too busy or too distracted to hear or listen.

Years back I had planned to purchase sixteen acres of land for a new ministry building. The day we were to sign the papers, I was hit hard in my spirit and clearly heard the Lord say, "Don't sign them. This is not the right place." I was upset and questioned, "Why didn't you tell me before we drew up these contracts?" I heard a strong rebuke, "I was trying to tell you, but you were too busy to hear me. You were doing what you wanted to do, and you were not still so I could speak to you." I rejected the purchase and later found the proper land on which to build the Omega Center International.

The lesson here is to stop and listen. A sudden burden is a signal to stop, listen, and pray. It could be a warning about a wrong decision or plan you are making. Don't let someone talk you out of paying attention to the inner pressing of your mind and spirit. Listen to the still small voice that is saying, "Don't go. Don't proceed with your plan."

Heeding the burden and obeying God's voice might just save your life or someone else's. When something terrible happens, we might look back and remember that God attempted to stop us, just like with Dad and the deer in the road. He will try to stop or delay us when He knows what is ahead. But we must learn to listen and discern the voice of God.

In the early 1980s I was driving alone early on a Sunday morning from Northport, Alabama to Jackson, Mississippi to preach. I was sleepy and for a moment I fell asleep. Suddenly I felt a hand strike me on my shoulder from the back seat, which startled me awake just in time to see that I was headed for the corner of a bridge. I jerked the steering wheel to get my car back on the highway. A fear of the Lord overwhelmed me, as I knew that was an angel of the Lord. I recalled how the angel smote Peter on his side to wake him up in the prison cell (Acts 12:7).

In Daniel 3:28, when the three Hebrew men were delivered from the fiery furnace, King Nebuchadnezzar said, "Blessed be the God of Shadrach, Meshach, and Abed-Nego, who sent His Angel and delivered His servants who trusted in Him, and they have frustrated the king's word, and yielded their bodies, that they should not serve nor worship any god except their own God!" In Daniel 6:22, when Daniel spent a night in the lion's dean and was not devoured, he told the king, "My God has sent his angel to shut the lions' mouths, that they have not hurt me: forasmuch as before him innocency was found in me..."

In the situation with Dad's half-brother Morgan, his backslidden condition and the fact that he had willfully walked away from the protective covering of Christ's blood meant that he had no angelic protection. However, through Dad's intercession on behalf of Morgan, the angel that had been assigned to Dad was able to prevent Morgan's premature death. This incident shook Morgan to the core. After Dad's death and just days before Morgan's own death, Morgan confessed Christ again, after wasting almost his entire life.

When I pray for my wife, children or grandchildren, I always ask God to send our generational angel to protect them if He sees danger or trouble ahead. Since our prayers are stored in golden vials in heaven (Rev. 5:8), I also pray this to ensure that this petition to God is ever before His throne. When traveling by plane, we always pray before takeoff that God will protect the plane and the pilot, and that He will put angels in front and behind to do as Joshua said, "to make our journey prosperous" by protecting us. It is good to read and claim biblical promises, such as the protective Psalm 91, over yourself and your family before you embark on any journey.

CHAPTER 20

SINNING CHRISTIANS: DELIVERED TO THE WILL OF SATAN

There are sins committed *before* and sins committed *after* a person is converted. John wrote that after we receive Christ, we are to *sin not*, or more literally, *cease from practicing a sinful lifestyle.* John also noted that, if anyone sins, we have an Advocate with the Father, Jesus Christ the righteous (1 John 2:1).

What about a Christian who knowingly sins, but ignores or delays repenting and asking God to cleanse them from their sins? What if the sin being committed also influences others to participate in the same sin? What if the sin is causing weak believers to turn away from Christ because the sin is corrupting the congregation?

Depending on the kind of sin and its impact on the congregation, Paul's answer might have been to turn the individual who is sinning over to Satan.

Why would Satan be involved in this process? Rabbinical Jewish thought concerning God's purpose for Satan is sometimes different from traditional Christian theology. Christians view Satan as the accuser, the tempter, a deceiver, and a slanderer—descriptions that identify his character throughout scripture.

Rabbis, on the other hand, see Satan as a potential agent of God. For example, in Job's story, Satan becomes an agent of God in testing Job. Satan could move against Job only with God's permission. Satan's involvement in sin, as well as the judgment God releases against a sin, can be explained in some verses written by Paul, a former Jewish rabbi and an expert in the law and traditions of the Jews. Paul wrote:

"And a servant of the Lord must not quarrel but be gentle to all, able to teach, patient, in humility correcting those who are in opposition, if God perhaps will grant them repentance, so that they may know the truth, and that they may come to their senses and escape the snare of the devil, having been taken captive by him to do his will."

— 2 TIMOTHY 2:24-26 (NKJV)

The story behind this verse is that Timothy, Paul's spiritual son, was being challenged by elders within his congregation. They were instigating a controversy, claiming that Timothy was too young and inexperienced to pastor such an older, mature congregation. The uprising had generated contention and sharp division within the church, thereby opening a door for Satan to take advantage of the people who were quarreling. Paul considered this outbreak of internal fighting a "snare (trap) of the devil." Only when his accusers repented and came to the knowledge of the truth could they escape the spiritual captivity of the enemy.

Sometimes when a person is causing division or trouble, someone will say they have "lost all common sense." Paul prayed that those verbally attacking this young pastor would come to their senses, as their actions were playing into the will of Satan, who is always the author of confusion in the church (1 Cor. 14:33).

The Jewish branch of the first century church was familiar with the laws in the Torah, which detailed God's firm opposition to sin and disobedience. The devout Jews who converted to Christianity required no training on what was right and wrong. The Gentiles who received Christ were a different story because most had been pagans and idolators. The Gentile cities were infested with idolatry, prostitution, orgies, drunkenness, extortion, and unjust judges. Paul noted the past sins of the new followers of Christ:

> *"Do you not know that the unrighteous will not inherit the kingdom of God? Do not be deceived. Neither fornicators, nor idolaters, nor adulterers, nor homosexuals, nor sodomites, nor thieves, nor covetous, nor drunkards, nor revilers, nor extortioners will inherit the kingdom of God. And such were some of you. But you were washed, but you were sanctified, but you were justified in the name of the Lord Jesus and by the Spirit of our God."*
>
> – 1 Cᴏʀɪɴᴛʜɪᴀɴs 6:9-11 (NKJV)

At times Christians would sin, and the sin would be known among the congregants. On more than one occasion, when individuals were guilty of unrepentant sin, Paul suggested they be "turned over to Satan for the destruction of their flesh." The following verse shows how Paul dealt with two men hindering the Gospel. The statement was written in Paul's first letter to Timothy:

> *"Of whom are Hymenaeus and Alexander; whom I have delivered unto Satan, that they may learn not to blaspheme."*
>
> – 1 Tɪᴍᴏᴛʜʏ 1:20 (NKJV)

Hymenaeus was publicly denying the resurrection of the dead (2 Tim. 2:17-18), causing some new believers to lose faith. Alexander was likely the coppersmith who did Paul much harm (2 Tim. 4:14). It appears that both men had once experienced faith in Christ, yet both became shipwrecked in their faith by rejecting sound doctrine.

A person cannot be a half-believer, accepting the parts of truth they choose and rejecting the parts they disapprove of.

This same method was used by Paul at the church in Corinth, Greece. Here was Paul's advice:

> "In the name of our Lord Jesus Christ, when you are gathered together, along with my spirit, with the power of our Lord Jesus Christ, deliver such a one to Satan for the destruction of the flesh, that his spirit may be saved in the day of the Lord Jesus."
>
> – 1 CORINTHIANS 5:4-5 (NKJV)

This was written to address a bizarre situation that had unfolded at a church in Corinth. A single man was committing fornication with his stepmother (his father's wife). The church knew about it, yet they were allowing it.

Turning the disobedient over to Satan for the destruction of their flesh was introduced to the church by Paul. We know what happens when a protective hedge is lifted (as with Job, see Job 1:10). Once Paul's apostolic authority was released in the church, God removed His protective hand and Satan was permitted to inflict suffering on the young man.

Eventually the young man must have repented, since Paul told the church that the punishment was sufficient, and the young man should now be forgiven and comforted, "lest he be swallowed up in much sorrow" (2 Cor. 2:7). "Swallowed up" is the same phrase used when referring to Satan being a roaring lion seeking whom he may devour (1Pet 5:8). The words *swallow up* and *devour* are the same in Greek, and the words mean "overwhelmed, drowned, to gulp down." The imagery is a lion eating a victim down to the bone and then slurping up any remains. It does not just refer to a satanic attack, but the intent of utter destruction. Satan was permitted to inflict some type of physical, mental, or emotional crisis on the young man to humble him to repentance.

The purpose was to produce this outcome: that in the end his soul might be saved in the day of the Lord Jesus Christ (1 Cor. 5:5). The *end* could allude to him returning to Christ at the end of this crisis or at the end of his life, if he repented. Without repentance, the young man in the church at Corinth would have been in serious eternal danger.

The soul refers to the eternal soul that dwells in the physical body. It can be saved only when one repents, turns from wickedness, and comes back to God. To be saved is *sozo,* which can refer to being healed, delivered, protected, and made whole.

This narrative indicates that God can and will permit certain negative situations to happen in the life of a disobedient person, in order that the person might return to Him. In the three biblical cases discussed here, the purpose was not that God would kill these three men, but that they would experience adversity and repent, so that in the end their souls would be saved. God desires that nobody perish and that all come to Him through repentance.

Paul's boldness to execute a chastisement upon those willfully sinning was not a response to personal anger or pride to demonstrate his apostolic authority. It was in hope that these disobedient men, after enduring a season of pain and sorrow, would repent, turn from the sin, and be restored to full salvation.

The second reason was that, if these sins were known and permitted to continue within the church, others in the assembly could have been tempted by the same sin, thereby giving them a false sense that their disobedience would go unchallenged and unpunished. In Acts 5, when Ananias and Sapphira lied to Peter, both were struck dead and buried the same day. Word spread, causing great fear of God to overtake the church.

This action of being "turned over to Satan" applies in the case where an individual's flagrant sin is known in the congregation, but the congregation is allowing it. Secondly, it applies if the sin is impacting others within the congregation.

Once the person has been turned over, chastisement or judgment will begin. The result that God desires is repentance and turning from wickedness. If the person repents and has a contrite spirit, then with the agreement of the leadership, they are to be restored back into the assembly of believers.

It is best for Christians to deal with all their sin issues than to face this type of chastisement.

SUFFERING LEADING TO REPENTANCE

Several times I have asked people in conferences what brought them to the place of repentance and receiving Christ. Some were raised in church and had received Christ at a young age. Others indicated they were won to Christ by a family member or a close friend. However, sometimes as many as half of those present confessed that they turned to the Lord after a sudden tragedy, a serious trial, or a crisis that struck them or their family. The crisis awakened their spirit to turn to God.

Suffering is never pleasant, and extreme trouble is not something anyone would choose. However, at times God will use a crisis to open the heart and intellect of a person who had been paying no attention to eternal things. Many times, someone who never prays will find themselves praying when they are hanging by a thread between life and death.

Two thieves illustrate this point. On one cross, to the left of Christ, was a thief. His partner in crime was on Christ's right side. One thief was self-serving, demanding that if Jesus really is the Messiah, He should prove it by getting him off the cross and sparing his life. The other thief knew that he would soon die, yet he petitioned Christ to let him into the eternal kingdom. In extreme suffering, there were two reactions. One was compliant and the other was defiant. Suffering hardened one man while it softened the heart of another. One was focused on his earthy life, but the other on eternal life.

When a person comes close to death, or when a sudden death occurs, both the converted and unconverted become aware of their own mortality. This can serve as an open door to remind the unconverted that heaven is reserved for those whose names are in the book of life, and the time for making a decision about eternity is now; not later.

Each personal trial has both a purpose and a conclusion. Although we might form in our minds an anticipated outcome, God has already prepared a way of escape for you (1 Cor. 10:13). Sometimes Christian sheep stray from the path of a protective shepherd and from the way of righteousness. God provides each prodigal a space of time to return to the fold. This requires a U-turn, at which point you return to the faith you walked away from. If our space of time runs out, without God's intended results, then the Almighty will act in a more severe manner (Rev. 2:21-23).

The fear of God (reverence and reverent submission) assists us as a restraining force. Growing up, I did not want to miss the coming of Christ. The thought of being left behind motivated me to follow the Lord, especially in my teen years, keeping my heart tender toward the Lord. In my mature years, the reality of mortality, knowing that I could die before Christ returns, helps me every day to cling closer to God and less to the world.

JEZEBEL IN THE CHURCH

One of the significant warnings that God gave the church is found in Revelation 2:20-23. The woman mentioned is a self-acclaimed prophetess named Jezebel. Some scholars believe she was the wife of the Bishop of Thyatira. One of her sins was teaching people to eat food sacrificed to idols. Another sin was seducing the men serving in the church to commit fornication.

She was given a space to repent (Rev. 2:21). The Greek word here for space is *chronos*, which is a specific set time for an event or opportunity. There is not a specific time frame linked with a "space" of time. It could vary by person and circumstance; but using a biblical reference point, the time frame could be between six months and one year.

King Nebuchadnezzar was warned that God would judge him if he did not humble himself and repent. Daniel implored the king, "Break off your sins and iniquities; show mercy to the poor..." (Dan. 4:27). One year later, the king experienced a severe mental breakdown that persisted without relief for seven years. We read: "And at the end of days I Nebuchadnezzar lifted up mine eyes unto heaven, and my understanding returned unto me..." (Dan. 4:34).

The king's trial was long; but in the end, the destruction of his flesh led to his repentance. He returned to his right mind and gave God glory.

God said that He gave Jezebel time to repent, but she did not do so. The process of God dealing with her would include casting her into a bed of sickness, and anybody who committed adultery with her into great tribulation unless they repent of their deeds. Next would be the death of her children.

The warnings from God were meant to bring a fear of the Lord upon the congregation, and for the churches to "know that I am He who searches the minds and hearts" (Rev. 2:23). The congregation would then understand the importance of walking in obedience to God and rejecting a life of sin.

INFLUENCING OTHERS TO SIN

A globally recognized contemporary ministry that was known for their music, large churches, and gifted preachers was also known for drinking all forms of alcoholic beverages after their church services.

They called this "liberty." Friends of mine who ministered at some of their campus churches refused to participate in their free-style drinking. On one occasion, a female minister was almost harassing a non-drinking female teacher for not drinking with the worship team.

When I heard about their drunken escapades, I warned visiting ministers that this is not pleasing to God. They should shun the appearance of evil and not let their good be evil spoken of, not to mention being a stumbling block to former alcoholics. This had to catch up with them at some point. Eventually it did.

My missionary friend Rusty Dominque made an observation. He said, "It is one thing when an individual sins, but it is another thing to try to make someone else sin. When this happens, God Himself will get involved and bring chastisement or judgment."

One verse explains, "Some men's sins are clearly evident, preceding them to judgment, but those of some men follow later" (1 Tim. 5:24). Some sins will be revealed on earth, giving the person the opportunity to repent and turn before they stand before God at the judgment. For others, their sin remains concealed on earth but will follow them to the judgment seat of Christ and be revealed at that time.

THE FOURFOLD PROCESS

If a Christian is battling a powerful bondage and is stuck in repetitive cycles of transgression, there is often a four-part process that God allows to bring them to a crisis point, then hopefully to repentance and deliverance from the sin.

The first step is *conviction*. Holy Spirit conviction is a strong inner feeling that wrong has been done, as the Holy Spirit deals with the conscience of the person. This feeling is described as heaviness in the heart and a weight pressing on the conscience, bringing the heart and mind to a crossroads.

The flesh (carnal) nature will whisper that you should ignore conviction, and even falsely try to convince you that it is all right to continue in this transgression. Meanwhile, the Spirit of the Lord is pressing you to repent and turn from the transgression. Conviction is the evidence of a clash between two kingdoms and a battle between the will of God and your carnal will.

If the sin is glossed over and continues, the second phase happens when God provides *a space of time for repentance* and for resisting the pressure to continue in a transgression. The woman called Jezebel is an example. She was sinning and influencing others to sin, and she was given a "space to repent." This space of time could vary, depending upon the seriousness of the transgression and how it is impacting others.

If a space of time to repent is ignored, God's next step is *chastisement*. The New Testament Greek word means "to learn instruction by disciplinary action." It is a word used when a parent firmly corrects an erring child as a form of discipline. Chastisement is when God corrects a person using a more intense, personal process.

Job 34:30 notes that, "The hypocrite should not reign, lest the people be ensnared." One person's sin can also ensnare another person who participates with them. Youth often pressure other youth to try illegal drugs or drink alcoholic beverages. This can lead to drunkenness, which can lead to vehicle accidents, arguments and fights, or having a driver's license revoked. The consequence of certain behaviors could be time spent in prison. Some men who are presently incarcerated have written letters to tell me that God likely saved their life through prison by getting them off the street and away from criminal behavior.

If chastisement is ignored, then the person is in danger of a selective form of *judgment*. This is the level of turning someone over to Satan for the destruction of their flesh. God warned Jezebel that if she persisted in her sin and did not repent, God would cast her in a bed of tribulation, and she would see her children slain. This was a targeted judgment that would put an end to Jezebel's influence and seduction of men in the church.

Notice each gradual process. As often said, God visits in mercy before He visits in judgment. Mercy triumphs over judgment (James 2:13).

I must make one thing abundantly clear. Just because a Christian experiences a terrible situation, such as a disease, a sudden death, or a terrible accident, is not an indicator that God was punishing them. These things happen to everybody, including sinners, because it rains on the just and the unjust. This four-step process is simply a method that God uses because He is concerned about everyone's eternal soul, and He desires that no one perish, but that everyone come to repentance. He will sometimes go to extreme measures to ensure that people turn to Him and secure eternal salvation of their soul in the end.

REMOVING THE SOURCE

There have been situations in which an unsaved young person pulled a Christian young person into a lifestyle of sin. The parents of the Christian young person were grieved, and they continually prayed that God would intervene or separate their child from the one who led them down a dark path. I have known of several cases in which the unsaved individual died suddenly, thereby causing an abrupt separation between the two. In the cases involving drugs, it is possible that the separation spared the other person from a premature death by stopping the influencer, who kept the victim connected to them through use of drugs.

Remember that God allows a space for people to repent and change their direction. If the people persist in sin and refuse to repent, they risk being severely judged by God Himself.

DESIRING FREEDOM BUT STRUGGLING

People react to sins and bondages in different ways. Consider the common destructive addictions in our culture—drugs, alcohol, and pornography.

One person might accept the addiction as part of life and continually feed their cravings without remorse and with no desire for freedom or deliverance.

Another person doesn't constantly feed an addiction, but they can't give it up completely. They vacillate between abstinence and returning to the sin for an occasional quick fix. Their behavior might be influenced by people or circumstances. These people might still sense conviction that brings a feeling of remorse for their actions. However, with the return of strong temptation, the person once again will partake of the bondage.

A third group sincerely desires to be free. They use spiritual tools, counseling, and whatever means available to help themselves gain victory over their addiction. This is the group that receives freedom because they have the mind, will, and desire to be set free.

A believer in Christ should be quick to repent and strive to be an overcomer. The objective is not to be the fastest person in the race, but to cross the finish line as a victorious Christian. The speed of the race will vary with different people, but God is concerned about how things *end*.

THE SIN UNTO DEATH

One of the most perplexing scriptures in the New Testament is found in the book of First John:

> *"If anyone sees his brother sinning a sin which does not lead to death, he will ask, and He will give him life for those who commit sin not leading to death. There is sin leading to death. I do not say that he should pray about that. All unrighteousness is sin, and there is sin not leading to death."*
>
> – 1 JOHN 5:16-17 (NKJV)

This might be one of the most difficult passages to interpret in the New Testament. To understand these verses, I used the *Adam Clark Biblical Commentary*, along with my own notes, to help explain the three most common interpretations of John's statement.

One interpretation is that some sins in the Bible were assigned the punishment of death—idolatry, incest, murder, and so on. Other sins did not require the penalty of death, such as sins committed inadvertently or out of ignorance. In their own nature, these sins appear to be comparatively light and trivial. Such distinctions existed in the Torah laws. A sin unto death was punishable by stoning (such as blasphemy in Leviticus 24:16), while a sin not unto death required the guilty person to bring a trespass offering at the temple (Lev. 4:2-18). Thus, there were sins unto death and sins not unto death.

A second interpretation of the verses involves transgressions of the civil laws of a nation or city. Some crimes are punishable with death, under which the person might be sentenced according to a legally recognized death penalty. In such cases, once guilt is proven and appeals have been made, prayers generally cannot change the outcome of the punishment. There are civil cases in which a crime was committed that is not punishable by death, and through prayer and intercession the person might be spared by a minor punishment that eventually leads to a release from the past activity.

A third interpretation of a sin unto death means a case of transgression which God determines should be punishable by physical death. At the same time, God might extend mercy to the repentant soul.

An example is the disobedient prophet in 1 Kings 13:1-32 who strayed from God's specific instructions and suddenly was killed by a lion. Also, Ananias and Sapphira were church members, but both lied to the Holy Spirit and were struck dead by "a sin unto death." Nobody attempted to raise them from the dead, as they did with Dorcas (Acts 9:36-41), as this couple was under a divine punishment.

Using this interpretation, the sin not unto death is any sin which God does not choose to punish with death.

Others have suggested that the sin unto death refers to the unpardonable sin of blaspheming the Holy Spirit, as this is the only sin listed in the Bible that is not forgivable (Matt. 12:31-32). Before Paul's conversion, he admitted to forcing many of the Christians he arrested to blaspheme the Lord. He also stated that he was able to obtain mercy from God because he did these things in ignorance (1 Tim. 1:13). If a person has knowledge, yet accuses the Holy Spirit's work of being demonic, this is blasphemy, and they have sentenced themselves to eternal retribution by the words of their own mouth. If, as Paul, a person blasphemes in ignorance of the truth, prayer may be able to spare them from the sin unto death, if they repent.

LIVING SIN FREE IS THE KEY

In John 5, Christ healed a paraplegic man at the pool of Bethesda who had an infirmity, a physical weakness that had caused paralysis for thirty-eight years. After being instantly made well, Jesus gave the man an unusual warning:

> *"Afterward Jesus found him in the temple, and said to him, "See, you have been made well. Sin no more, lest a worse thing come upon you."*
>
> — JOHN 5:14 (NKJV)

This warning indicates that, when a person has been forgiven and healed, they must separate from a life of sin, or a worse thing could come upon them. Since Jesus spoke of sin and sinning no more, the clear implication is that this weakness had come upon the man after he became involved in some unnamed sin.

What did Jesus mean when He said that a worse thing would come upon him, if he returned to a sinful lifestyle after being made well? Some scholars suggest that a worse type of infirmity would return, while others suggest that what would be worse would be a return to sin and an eventual death that separates him from God in hell.

When a person has been redeemed from their sins and becomes a new creation in Christ, God gives them a season of grace and mercy after their conversion. Sometimes they don't yet understand that they cannot continue to return to their old ways and their former lifestyle. However, if the person continues in sin, there is often a chastisement or some type of divine judgment that forces the person to look to God for help.

God may allow some to be taken from earth while they are presently serving the Lord and ready to meet Him. Only God knows what might lie ahead if He allows them to live more years. A weakness of the flesh might re-emerge in the future, thereby opening a door to a lifestyle of sin that would jeopardize their eternal destiny. It is better for a person to pass away while they are young in their faith than to die in their sins at some point in the future.

It is prudent to deal with all sin while you are living, while you can obtain forgiveness and serve Christ, than to face those sins at the judgment seat of Christ. Today is the day to repent, turn, and follow Christ with your whole heart.

CHAPTER 21

DEATH CAN'T CHANGE
THE VERB

Death tends to change the verb. We speak in terms of "is," and then we speak in terms of "was." We hear the change immediately when we learn of the death of someone we know. From our exit from the womb to our entrance to the tomb, our name remains but the verb changes.

The word *is* identifies the living. She *is* a great person. He *is* a great business administrator. He *is* a great pastor. At death, she *was* a great person. He *was* a great pastor. Present tense identifies that the person is alive, while past tense indicates that the person's life has ended.

Human life ends and the person's breath has ceased. But death cannot change the verb!

I had never thought of that until it rose in my spirit after my cousin's untimely death. I had been unable to attend Louanna's homegoing in West Virginia because we had already planned to leave the next day for a family cruise and could not alter the plans. Her death was such a shock that I struggled to function the following week, even though I should have been enjoying our vacation.

I began to receive texts from the pastor that read: "The family is holding up well. The viewing is packed out. She must have known hundreds of people. The line is all the way through the church and out in the parking lot with no parking places to be found. What a legacy she is leaving. Wow."

That warmed my heart thinking that Lu always did things big—big plans, big ideas, and now having one of the biggest viewings the town had ever seen.

A few minutes later, Pastor Mike texted, "She touched so many people. I am amazed at how many folks have shown up!"

Louanna cared for everybody in life, and in turn, everyone honored her in death. The pastor was in awe of the love that people were showing, as he never realized her broad influence in Randolph and Tucker counties. So many people were showing up to give honor to the sister, aunt, cousin, co-worker, and friend who had shown so much care and love to them.

That's when I heard this statement in my spirit: Death cannot change the verb! The Holy Spirit continued to speak to my spirit: "You speak of her in the past tense, but she is more alive now than she was on earth. Her *was* does not exist because she still lives. To be absent from the body is to be present with the Lord" (2 Cor. 5:6).

When a person passes away, their lifeless body remains on the earth, but their spirit, which is very much alive, makes a journey to another world and another dimension of time. Right now we are too far away to see our loved ones and too divided by time and space to communicate with them. When David's infant son died, David stated, "Can I bring him back again? I shall go to him, but he shall not return to me" (2 Sam. 12:23).

STILL ALIVE ON THE OTHER SIDE

Heaven has three levels: the area of the clouds, the cosmic heavens, and an upper celestial realm that Paul called the third heaven (2 Cor. 12:2). In this third heavenly dimension is an area identified as paradise. This is the heavenly garden where the souls and spirits of those who trusted Christ for their salvation and served Him on earth are fully alive in spirit form. They have the same five senses and can recognize people who have gone on to heaven, as we will be known in heaven as we were known on earth (1 Cor. 13:12).

Every person who died in Christ is not identified as *was* (past tense), but as *are* (present tense). They *are* with the Lord. They *are* in Paradise. They *are* awaiting the resurrection of the dead. They *are* resting in the Lord and have ceased from their labors.

Jesus told us, "And if I go and prepare a place for you, I will come again and receive you to Myself; that where I am, there you may be also" (John 14:3). On a day unknown to each of us and known only to God, our earth's clock will expire. We will enjoy one last day, one last hour, and one final minute before we exhale one final breath. Then our body will release our eternal soul and spirit.

If you resisted God and refused to repent, you will begin a decent into a tunnel of darkness, into the eternal land of the lost. If you have received Christ, served Him, and followed His Word, you will ascend upward and quickly enter a land of eternal life and love in the paradise of God.

Before the passing of my dear cousin, our immediate family had never experienced the premature death of a family member who is close to us. In our generation, close family who died had been blessed to live a good, long life. Louanna's death was such a sudden shock, it alerted me once again to a timeless truth. There is no guarantee of tomorrow for any of us. The pale horse of death can gallop in your direction without you ever hearing his distant hoof beats. Today is the day of *your salvation*, as tomorrow may never come. In twenty-four hours, everything can change.

CHAPTER 22

ETERNITY IS IN YOUR HEART

By the time we reach a certain age, most of us awaken to an old reality that is based upon specific scriptures, such as Ecclesiastes 3:11: "He has made everything beautiful in its time. Also he has put eternity in their hearts...."

The sense of eternity that lurks inside each person will surface with passing time. This is why a person who has matured with age will start thinking about the important questions. What happens at death? Is there something beyond this life? What happens to my soul when I die? Is there a heaven and a hell?

Now that I've entered my senior years, I sense a greater connection to two worlds: this world and the world to come.

In Isaiah 57:15, God identifies himself as "the high and lofty one that inhabits eternity." Again, eternity means a *perpetual duration*, a time that is *everlasting*, such as "everlasting life" and "everlasting punishment" (John 3:16; Matt. 25:41). Everlasting has no end. Eternity past is identified as "times past" (Eph. 2:3), and eternity future is called "the ages to come" (Eph. 2:7).

Jesus did not come from the eternal realm of heaven for the purpose of starting a new religion called Christianity. He descended to earth through immaculate conception, born of a virgin, and shed His blood to forgive the sins of all who will repent and ask His forgiveness, so He can cleanse them from all unrighteousness.

Once we repent and receive forgiveness, we are rewarded with the gift of eternal life through Jesus Christ our Lord. The transformation that emerges from the heart of a repentant person includes making them a new creation, with a new path of thinking that begins to change their behavior.

There are two paths to follow. One path is narrow, and the other is wide. One leads to eternal life, and one leads to eternal destruction. *You alone own the choice. You decide where you will be for eternity.*

God gave you a human will with the ability and power to choose your own eternal destination. He has not handpicked some for heaven and others for hell, for His Word tells us that He is longsuffering toward us, not willing that *any* should perish but that *all* should come to repentance (2 Peter 3:9). God loved the world so much that He gave His only begotten Son, that whoever believes in Him should not perish but have everlasting life. God sent His Son here, not to condemn the world, but so that the world might be saved through Him (John 3:16-17).

Greek scholar Rick Renner explains "world" (kosmos in Greek) in this manner: the arena where Satan invades and attempts to wield his influence; where people do not live by the standard of God's Word; where ethics change with the times; the sphere where you have influence. Mark 16:15 tells us to go into all the world (kosmos) and preach the Gospel to every creature.

God's desire is that you receive salvation and everlasting life. It is my heart's desire as an evangelist that you know, without a doubt, where you will live for eternity. Choose life through Christ. Tomorrow is never promised. Today is the day of salvation (2 Cor. 6:2).

Pray this prayer sincerely from your heart:

"Heavenly Father, I come to you in the name of your Son, Jesus Christ. I approach you today as a sinner without a Savior. I believe in my heart that Jesus Christ is the Son of God who came

to redeem me from my sins through His blood on the cross. Right now, I ask you to forgive me of all my sins. Cleanse my body, soul, and spirit with the blood of Jesus. I confess that you are my Lord and Savior. Come and dwell in me right now. Thank you for your salvation. Help me to learn more about you, trust in you, pray to you, and worship you. Amen."

If you prayed this prayer and you sincerely meant it, you now have received the gift of eternal life. This is just the beginning of the rest of your new life. Here are four other steps to help you along the way:

- Find a good, Bible believing church where you can learn the word, grow in faith, and make new friends.

- Get baptized in water, as the Bible teaches, "Repent and be baptized" (Acts 2:38).

- Study the Word of God, as this will build your faith and help you discover amazing life truths.

- Pray every day and learn to worship the Lord.

If you have prayed this prayer to receive Christ, please contact our office at Voice of Evangelism and tell us by calling (423) 478-3456 or e-mailing us at voe@voe.org.

The International School of the Word offers a free course for you called New Believer's Handbook. This will help you start your new journey in Christ. The free course can be accessed by going to the International School of the Word website and looking for "New Believer's Handbook." The course can be found at this link: https://isow.org/courses/new-believers-handbook/.

By God's grace, one day we will see each other here, there, or in the air at Christ's return.

This book details stories from a world without time. Discover a world unseen, yet existing, as you expound on your knowledge of heaven and its inhabitants.

SECRETS of the THIRD HEAVEN

How to Find the Map Leading to Your Eternal Destination

PERRY STONE

DISCOVER THE ROADMAP TO HEAVEN!

BK-028 | $20

ORDER ONLINE AT PERRYSTONE.ORG

OR CALL (423) 478.3456